QUO VADIMUS

1st Edition August 2022

If you find an error in this book, please email support@quovadimusmedia.co.uk, with a description of the error and the page number.

About Quo Vadimus Media Ltd

We are a learning & media company based in the United Kingdom, using evidence-informed practice to help individuals and businesses to learn and improve in a changing world. We bring a wealth of knowledge from schools, colleges, universities and academic research to improve learning.

Our services and products are based on and developed from over 25 years of experience in the self-improvement and education sectors.

We provide online learning as well as producing print & digital publications to enhance learning and retention of knowledge.

Website: https://quovadimusmedia.co.uk

About the Author

Graeme Lamb is the founding Director of Quo Vadimus Media Ltd, a lecturer in accountancy at a college of Further Education in the northwest of England, and a practising bookkeeper holding AATQB (qualified bookkeeper) status with the AAT.

Table of Contents

Chapter	Page
1 - Introduction & Scenario *Bookkeeping, types of accounting, introduction to the scenario.*	1
2 - Starting the Business *Opening entries, assets and liabilities, bank and cash accounts, coding principles, double-entry bookkeeping, accounting equation, balancing accounts, VAT, digital focus.*	15
3 - Credit Purchases *Purchases documents and document-checking, trade and bulk discounts, prompt payment discounts, VAT, double-entry bookkeeping, daybooks (purchases, purchases returns, discounts received), digital focus.*	46
4 - Credit Sales *Double-entry bookkeeping, daybooks (sales, sales returns), prompt payment discounts, VAT, digital focus.*	87
5 – The Cash Book *Bank and cash accounts, cash book, petty cash book, daybooks (discounts allowed, discounts received), introduction to payment methods, digital focus.*	114
6 - The Petty Cash Book *Petty cash book, VAT, double-entry bookkeeping, digital focus.*	148
7 - Assessment Support *Before the assessment, the AAT examiner report, during the assessment.*	169
8 - Answers *Answers to chapter questions.*	173

Available from Quo Vadimus Media Ltd

All products are available from Amazon. Some products are also available from https://www.quovadimusmedia.co.uk.

Online guides are available from: https://learning.quovadimusmedia.co.uk.

General

Maths for Accounting (Levels 1 & 2) Online Edition *(online – available as a separate purchase)*

Level 1

Award in Bookkeeping Study Guide *(print and Kindle)*
Award in Bookkeeping: Online Guide/Revision Course *(online)*

Level 2

Introduction to Bookkeeping Study Guide *(print and Kindle)*
Introduction to Bookkeeping Skills and Knowledge Tests *(print and Kindle)*
Introduction to Bookkeeping Pocket Revision Guide *(print and Kindle)*

Principles of Bookkeeping Controls Study Guide *(print and Kindle)*
Principles of Bookkeeping Controls Skills and Knowledge Tests *(print and Kindle)*
Principles of Bookkeeping Controls Pocket Revision Guide *(print and Kindle)*

Principles of Costing Study Guide *(print and Kindle)*
Principles of Costing Skills and Knowledge Tests *(print and Kindle)*
Principles of Costing Pocket Revision Guide *(print and Kindle)*

The Business Environment Study Guide *(print and Kindle)*
The Business Environment Skills and Knowledge Tests *(print and Kindle)*

Introduction

The role of a **bookkeeper** is that of a faithful storyteller. A storyteller because a bookkeeper tells the story of a business by recording its financial transactions to indicate how the business is performing and what has been happening. Faithful, in that a good bookkeeper does so both honestly and accurately, complying with policies and legislation.

In studying the AAT Level 2 Certificate in Accounting, students become members of the AAT (Association of Accounting Technicians) and are bound by its Code of Professional Ethics, which can be found online.

This code follows five core principles:

- Integrity
- Objectivity
- Professional Competence and Due Care
- Confidentiality
- Professional Behaviour

The reputation of the AAT and the bookkeeping and accounting profession is dependent on workers within the profession working ethically and accurately.

This study guide is designed to allow students, whether starting out in the world of bookkeeping and accounting or already working within the industry, to develop their skills and knowledge as bookkeepers, with the ability to be faithful storytellers of the businesses for which they work and provide bookkeeping and accountancy services.

What is Bookkeeping?

Bookkeeping is about keeping the financial records of the business, in either a paper-based or computerised form. The practice of bookkeeping is governed by principles and practices that have developed over hundreds of years, as well as international standards and legislation.

A range of different approaches exist to bookkeeping, but throughout the world the most common system used is **double-entry bookkeeping**.

Bookkeeping also involves using the bookkeeping records to prepare end of year financial statements and accounts. Bookkeeping is part of what is known as **financial accounting**.

Accounting is separated into two main categories – financial and management.

Most of the units at level 2 & 3 involve financial accounting, whereas level 4 is predominantly management accounting.

Financial Accounting	Management Accounting
Financial accounting involves preparing materials for an external audience (e.g., HMRC, shareholders). Based on the financial activity of the business, recording transactions, and preparing financial statements. Is often based on international accounting standards and local legislation and must be produced to agreed standards (e.g., financial statements).	Management accounting involves preparing materials for an internal audience (e.g., managers, directors). Based on current trends, looking forward to the future (e.g., costing and budgeting). Is often based on international accounting standards but has more flexibility in how information is presented to internal audiences (e.g., monthly budget reports).

Although bookkeeping stretches back hundreds or even thousands of years to financial records of sales and purchases being recorded on stone or clay tablets, the more recent history of bookkeeping, before the technological progress allowed by computers in recent decades, meant that the financial records of businesses and individuals in business were often kept in a paper-based format.

Bookkeeping systems allowed for transactions to be recorded in a series of books known as **ledgers** that would record the transactions within a business over time. This allows for cross-referencing and tracking of information through a combination of coding practices and systems such as the use of double-entry.

In recent years, many businesses have transitioned to keeping their financial records digitally rather than on paper-based books or ledgers, although many businesses will still use a combination of paper and digital records for bookkeeping.

Most businesses have moved from using paper-based books and ledgers for keeping their records to using **accounting software**. In the United Kingdom, this has been recognised by **HMRC** (HM Revenue & Customs). This UK government department deals with the collection and administration of tax from individuals and businesses, as it requires more businesses over the coming years to comply with **Maxing Tax Digital**.

Maxing Tax Digital will require businesses to make their financial submissions to HMRC for **VAT** (Value Added Tax) and other matters using compatible digital software rather than paper-based returns and submissions, with few exceptions.

What is VAT?
VAT, more fully known as **Value Added Tax**, is an indirect tax on consumption that is charged on most goods and services. Businesses that are VAT-registered are required to charge VAT on goods and services that they sell according to the rules set down in the relevant government legislation. They must also provide a timely return to HMRC, which will result in either money paid to, or money reclaimed from HMRC. Details of such VAT returns are studied at level 3. There are several different VAT rates, but at level 2 students will either record transactions on which no VAT is to be charged or paid, or VAT is to be charged or paid at 20%.

Although many bookkeepers in the modern world are likely to be involved in computerised rather than manual bookkeeping and accounting, students and bookkeepers need to be aware of the manual processes that underpin bookkeeping rules and procedures, rather than just relying on the software to do the work for them.

This can be likened to the difference between being able to drive a car (computerised accounting) and being able to service and repair a car when problems arise, as well as having a deeper understanding of how it runs (manual accounting).

Modern, computerised accounting systems have various advantages over paper-based systems, including:

- Import transactions from numerous different sources, including bank records, CSV files (comma-separated values, often from spreadsheet programs), and other third-party software.
- The ability to automatically total and balance accounts.
- Automatically post from daybooks and other books of prime entry to the General Ledger.
- Automatically reconcile Receivables/Payables Ledgers to the relevant control accounts.
- Automatically generate a trial balance or audit trail.
- Process recurring entries.

However, disadvantages of these systems also can occur, created by:

- Misunderstanding of how the software works, or how data should be entered or imported.
- Errors in original documents.
- Errors in data entry by bookkeepers and accountants.

Information that is incorrectly entered, whether in a manual or digital bookkeeping system, can cause a cost to the business, both financial and in terms of reputation or lost business.

A change that AAT has brought in for the Q2022 qualification specification at level 2 is that although students should continue to be taught the manual processes that underpin bookkeeping knowledge, the computerised version of these processes and how they differentiate from their manual version is also considered at the same time, and students should practice both skills. However, only the manual processes are assessed, although theoretical knowledge of computerised accounting systems is assessed.

Each chapter in this book will follow this principle. Students will first be taught the manual processes that they will be required to know to demonstrate their knowledge and understanding of the various exam tasks. Students will also be shown how this may be similar or different when using modern computerised accounting software. This will be covered in the **Digital Focus** section at the end of each chapter.

No specific accounting software will be recommended here, as different training providers may have preferences as to what they use to teach students, and students who are learning through self-study may wish to discover the options for themselves.

It is however recommended that for the scenario that students will follow throughout the rest of this book, that computerised accounting software is available and accessible, and students could consider following along with the scenario that is outlined in this book, entering transactions themselves.

A word of warning. Many people embark on a period of studying bookkeeping thinking that they will enjoy it or be good at it as they are good at or enjoy maths.

Although the financial transactions of a business inevitably involve a certain amount of maths and arithmetic, the student should be advised that bookkeeping, particularly double-entry bookkeeping, is as much about rules and processes as it is about arithmetic.

Students must have a good grasp of English, particularly in terms of an ability to analyse and comprehend potentially complex lists of instructions.

The maths in level 2 bookkeeping is not particularly difficult, but what is difficult is understanding what maths to do at any given point and how to apply it to the rules of bookkeeping.

Scenario

Bookkeeping is often taught on a topic-by-topic basis, and that can be very effective. However, this book will teach bookkeeping using a different approach, where the materials for the whole unit will be taught not just through topics but as an ongoing case study. This will involve following an individual through the start of a new business and sharing their journey as they make a range of different transactions, buying and selling, investing money into the business, and paying expenses, over a set period of three months from January to March.

Through this case study, students will see many of the different aspects involved in bookkeeping in practice and see how different elements of the process, as well as the varying rules and procedures in bookkeeping, combine to tell the ongoing story of the business. This approach will enable students to see bookkeeping as part of a more comprehensive system, making it easier to understand the different rules as they are demonstrated.

Learning bookkeeping in this way makes it possible to see bookkeeping not as an abstract set of rules and procedures but within the context of a (fictional) business using real-world bookkeeping principles and practices.

Students will then be able to practice those same skills in a range of activities at the end of each chapter that will consolidate the skills and knowledge, using a variety of question styles that will help them prepare for their examination. These activities are unrelated to the scenario presented in the chapter, although they use the same bookkeeping principles.

The scenario constructed for this study is based on a new business owner, Morgan Rothby, who has set up a business making and selling bicycles.

The scenario will follow Megan through the early bookkeeping transactions of the business, buying from suppliers and selling to customers, and receiving and paying money in and out of the bank.

The scenario followed for this book and this unit is outlined on the next page.

Scenario

Morgan has started a business making and selling bicycles. This business is called Delta Q Bikes Ltd and makes both standard and electric bicycles. Bicycles are sold to shops, who then sell them on to customers, and are also sold direct to customers by Delta Q Bikes Ltd via their online shop and website.

Morgan has put some of her own money into the business (this is known as capital) as well as money from a friend and a bank loan (which are known as liabilities).

She has rented a property from which to manufacture bikes and store them in a warehouse and has hired two other employees. Morgan has also invested in specialist machinery (an asset) for manufacturing the bikes.

The business will use a double-entry bookkeeping system, which uses a series of day books (for credit sales and purchases) linked to a Receivables Ledger, a Payables Ledger, and the General Ledger.

The business will buy components and other items from suppliers, which are known as credit purchases, and will sell finished goods to shops, which are known as credit sales.

Cash sales to retail customers, from the online website, are also recorded.

A Cash Book and Petty Cash book are used, both of which are books of prime entry and double-entry, and will record the money element of all purchases, expenses and income, as well as any drawings made by the owner.

This scenario will be repeated in full at the beginning of every chapter to remind students of the context. Throughout the study guide, students will be encouraged to follow the story of Morgan as she starts her business and to approach the learning from that perspective.

Various key terms have been outlined in this scenario. Although they will be examined in detail later, it is helpful to look at simple definitions now to begin understanding.

The definitions are in two categories:

- Sales & purchases
- Transaction locations

Sales & Purchases

Understanding the correct usage of the terms cash and credit is a vital part of understanding the basics of double-entry bookkeeping.

Care must be taken in this, as the use of these terms in accounting and bookkeeping often differs from how the terms may be used in standard English.

The word cash is typically understood to mean notes and coins. However, this is not always the case in accounting & bookkeeping.

Similarly, the use of the term credit must be understood within context. It does not indicate whether an entry should be a debit or credit within a particular account, in that all cash or credit transactions will involve both debit and credit entries.

The usage of the terms cash and credit within the context of sales and purchases usually refers to when payment is expected to take place.

Cash Sale	A sale that the business has made where payment has been made immediately.
Cash Purchase	A purchase that the business has made where payment has been made immediately.
Credit Sale	A sale where payment is made at a later date, according to payment terms set by the seller.
Credit Purchase	A purchase where payment is made at a later date, according to payment terms set by the seller.

Cash and credit sales and purchases may, or may not, be paid in cash. The terms cash and credit do not indicate the method of payment, only the time of payment.

Transaction Locations

Financial transactions will be recorded in a number of different locations, depending on the type and nature of the transaction.

Books of Prime Entry	The first place in the accounting system in which a financial transaction is recorded.
Day books	Books of prime entry for recording transactions around credit sales and credit purchases only.
Double-entry	The main bookkeeping of the accounting system for many businesses, recorded in individual accounts in what are known as ledgers, as described below.
Receivables Ledger	A collection of individual accounts (credit customers) to which the business has sold on credit.
Payables Ledger	A collection of individual accounts (credit suppliers) from which the business has bought on credit.
General Ledger	A collection of individual accounts for a variety of different types of transaction within the business, covering a range of transactions. Often numerically arranged in categories.

In the following chapters, the scenario will take students through a series of different processes that a business may go through, showing how the books of prime entry and double-entry bookkeeping work together to record the different financial transactions of the business.

Each chapter will introduce the key concepts involved in that chapter. As students work through the different chapters, they will see the financial transactions of the business as it records initial financial entries for the start of a business, buys from suppliers and sells to customers, and recording money coming in and out of the business.

At the end of each chapter there will be hints as to how these transactions can be entered into computerised accounting software.

Content & Style Notes

In this textbook, we have chosen to use the term day books rather than daybooks, although they are identical, and it is essentially a matter of style and preference.

Students will not notice that numbers are sometimes given with (1,000) or without (1000) comma separators. Either is common in bookkeeping, and either is acceptable in assessments, unless instructions say otherwise.

In this guide, day books will generally use numbers without comma separators, whereas ledger accounts will use numbers with comma separators. This is not intended to show any difference in behaviour between those two types of records, merely to show both methods in operation.

In some cases, the order in which transactions have been entered or listed in the various General Ledger accounts are changed in subsequent entries. This is to match date order and make the accounts as easily readable as possible for students. In manual accounting, transactions will generally be listed in the order they are entered, although that may lead to some transactions seeming out of order in terms of dates. By contrast, transactions entered in accounting software can easily be filtered by transaction date, rather than date of entry, which may not be the same.

Some accounts will be shown as balanced at the end of a month before further transactions are shown. This is done to more fully show that the case study takes place over a number of months, where accounts are likely to balance at regular intervals. Although this is demonstrated here, students are not expected to balance an account then add further transactions at level 2.

It is often advisable within accounting to track the progress of raw materials through to work-in-progress or finished goods in terms of inventory, to give a fuller picture of the value of the assets of the business. This is avoided here for simplicity, although this terminology will be considered more in the unit, Principles of Costing, and is also studied in detail at level 3.

This case study of the starting of a new business is of course only a snapshot, used and edited in order to teach the very basics of bookkeeping, and a real business startup may use a wider range of transactions with more detail. However, it is hoped that this scenario-based case study will help students with an introduction to the principles of bookkeeping.

Digital Focus

The advent of technology has meant that computerised accounting software has become a vital component in bookkeeping and accounting.

The history of bookkeeping and accounting has commonly meant keeping business records in a series of books or ledgers. As computers became more prevalent in the workplace, spreadsheets were increasingly used to record transactions and accounts and businesses sprang up providing financial and accounting software.

Until recently, most computerised accounting software involved installing an application onto a particular computer, and any records or transactions recorded in the computer could only be accessed on that computer, or a limited number of computers that were licensed to use the software.

Although backups of software and transactions could be exported and kept on floppy disks, backup cartridges or CD-ROMS, there was limited scope for using different computers to access the records of the business. Careful consideration needed to be given to backup policies and procedures to ensure that data was not lost or stolen, potentially threatening the ability of the business to record its bookkeeping transactions and keep required records.

The recent advent of cloud computing has meant that many accounting software providers are moving away from desktop-based software that requires installation on a particular computer, to web browser-based software that can be accessed from any computer and any user with access to the login details. Many cloud-based accounting software solutions now also have apps for mobile phones that enable access to a set of limited features on the move. This may include moving money between bank accounts, recording payments or receipts, and the ability to upload pictures of receipts and invoices. Careful consideration must be given to keeping passwords and access secure to avoid data loss or theft.

There are various software packages available, some of the most common in the UK currently being provided by Sage, FreeAgent, Xero and QuickBooks. Those software providers, and others, provide different versions of their products aimed at various business types, including sole traders, partnerships, limited companies and charities. Some larger businesses however may have software written especially for them.

Summary

Bookkeeping is part of financial accounting.

Bookkeeping involves recording the financial transactions of the business, often using a combination of the following:

- Day books
- General Ledger
- Receivables Ledger
- Payables Ledger
- Cash Book
- Petty Cash Book

A double-entry system is common in bookkeeping. Bookkeeping also often involves using the records from bookkeeping to produce end of year financial statements and company accounts.

The bookkeeping system allows for easy coding and cross-referencing that make it possible to track transactions and balances more easily.

Historically, this system has been paper-based and involved using books and ledgers to keep track of transactions and account balances.

This system, particularly since the advent of modern computerised accounting software, when accessed through desktop software or a web browser, is an efficient and effective way of recording and monitoring the progress of a business through its regular transactions.

Businesses will in the future be required to not only record their transactions and keep their accounts digitally, but to submit their accounts and VAT returns (if applicable) in an acceptable format for HMRC as part of **Making Tax Digital**.

Students will learn the manual processes that underpin bookkeeping with its rules and processes and their computerised counterparts.

Students should be aware that a good grasp of knowledge and comprehension of English is required to understand the complex rules and procedures, as well as understanding what is required from exam questions.

Skills & Knowledge Test – Chapter 1

QUESTION 1

Identify the following as either cash or credit transactions by ticking the appropriate box.

	Cash Sale	Cash Purchase	Credit Sale	Credit Purchase
A sale where payment is required at a later date as indicated by its payment terms.				
A purchase where immediate payment is required.				
A purchase where payment is required at a later date as indicated by its payment terms.				
A sale where immediate payment is required.				

QUESTION 2

Identify the purpose of each of these ledgers by ticking the appropriate box.

	Receivables Ledger	Payables Ledger	General Ledger
Contains the records of a number of different accounts for the business, dealing with a wide range of different transactions.			
Contains individual accounts for customers to whom the business sells on credit.			
Contains individual accounts for suppliers from whom the business buys on credit.			

QUESTION 3

Bookkeeping is part of.... *(tick as appropriate)*

Financial accounting	
Management accounting	

QUESTION 4

Identify the following by ticking the correct box.

	Ledger Accounts	Day books
The place where transactions are recorded or transferred to the double-entry accounting system.		
Books which are used for recording the initial transactions regarding credit sales and credit purchases.		

QUESTION 5

Match the accounting category to the description by putting the correct answer in the box.

Options: *capital, drawings, asset, liability, expense, income, purchase*

Running costs of the business.	
An amount of money owed by the business to a third party.	
Money received from the sale of goods.	
Money taken out of the business by the owner.	
An item of value owned by the business.	
Money spent on buying raw materials or finished goods for resale.	
Money put into the business by the owner.	

This section has been created for you should you wish to use it to make notes or for calculations.

Starting the Business

Introduction

Starting a business is a complex process involving numerous steps and should be carefully planned before execution.

Although much should be considered when starting a business, the sole focus in this study guide is on bookkeeping and financial transactions. Firstly, a reminder of the scenario:

Scenario
Morgan has started a business making and selling bicycles. This business is called Delta Q Bikes Ltd and makes both standard and electric bicycles. Bicycles are sold to shops, who then sell them on to customers, and are also sold direct to customers by Delta Q Bikes Ltd via their online shop and website. Morgan has put some of her own money into the business (this is known as capital) as well as money from a friend and a bank loan (which are known as liabilities). She has rented a property from which to manufacture bikes and store them in a warehouse and has hired two other employees. Morgan has also invested in specialist machinery (an asset) for manufacturing the bikes. The business will use a double-entry bookkeeping system, which uses a series of day books (for credit sales and purchases) linked to a Receivables Ledger, a Payables Ledger, and the General Ledger. The business will buy components and other items from suppliers, which are known as credit purchases, and will sell finished goods to shops, which are known as credit sales. Cash sales to retail customers, from the online website, are also recorded. A Cash Book and Petty Cash book are used, both of which are books of prime entry and double-entry, and will record the money element of all purchases, expenses and income, as well as any drawings made by the owner.

There are two presumptions to be made about Delta Q Bikes Ltd, Morgan's new business:

- That the bank account for the business has been set up and is ready to receive money and to make payments.
- That the business is **VAT-registered** from the outset. This is not always the case in the real world, as businesses are not required to register for VAT until the turnover has reached a certain level. Some businesses will choose to do so, as in this case, as it is advantageous to do so to reclaim VAT from HMRC paid out on purchases.

This chapter will look at various early transactions for the business, such as:

- The paying in of money by Morgan into the business to provide funds for **purchases** and **expenses**. This is Morgan's own money that she is providing and is known as **capital.** Capital is sometimes referred to as **equity**, particularly when referring to the value of shares held in a business.
- The paying in of money received because of a loan from the bank. This is money that is owed back to the bank and is known as a **liability**.
- The paying out of money because of buying equipment for making the bikes. These pieces of equipment are inventory that will have material value (**assets**) that can be recorded and are owned by the business.
- The paying out of money because of buying raw materials from which to build the bikes, which will be recorded as **purchases**.
- **Account coding** in the **General Ledger** in order to record these transactions, and the relationship between assets, liabilities and capital in the form of **the accounting equation.**
- How to balance accounts manually.

This will involve a basic introduction to some of the principles of double-entry bookkeeping, such as how cash and bank transactions are recorded, as well as different categories of transaction and how they differ from each other. Correctly recording transactions to be analysed within the bookkeeping and in any financial statements is a vital part of the bookkeeping process.

Double-Entry Bookkeeping

Double-entry bookkeeping is so-called for the following reasons:

- Each transaction is usually* recorded as a pair of entries.
- One entry will be in one account, whereas the second entry will be in another account.
- The two accounts involved will be determined by the nature of/reason for the transaction.
- One account will contain the debit entry, one account will contain the credit entry.
- The two sides must match, and the debit entry must equal the credit entry.

**In some cases, there will be three entries rather than two. This is often the case when there are transactions involving VAT.*

Accounts in the General Ledger, as well as those in the Receivables or Payables Ledger, are set out in what is known as a 'T' account format, with the **left-hand side for debit entries** and the **right-hand side for credit entries.** It is commonly the case the debit entry is entered before the credit entry, a convention that will often be followed in this book.

The debit side is often shortened to *dr*, from the Latin, *debitum*, whilst the credit side is often shortened to *cr*, from the Latin, *creditum*.

Debitum means 'what is due' and *creditum* means 'a loan, or entrusted to someone'. This correlates with what you will learn about assets and liabilities.

Below is an example of how a double-entry account may look, particularly in a manual, paper-based accounting system.

First is shown the name of the account, and in this case the Nominal (or General Ledger) code that has been assigned to it. It is common that bank and cash accounts will have numbers in the 1200 range.

Then the two sides are shown, the debit side on the left and the credit side on the right.

The exact layout will vary, and in your studies you are likely to see a variety of layouts, from the layouts in this guide to those in AAT practice questions and in computerised accounting software.

Bank Account (1200)			
Debit *(dr)*	£	Credit *(cr)*	£

There are two main rules for double-entry:

Rule 1 – involves the half of the double-entry transaction involving money coming in to or going out of the bank, or the cash coming into or going out of the business, and deals with the bank/cash half of the transaction.

Rule 2 – involves the other half of the transaction, involving asset, liability, expense, income, purchase, capital or drawings accounts. This rule would also apply when money is not changing hands at that time. Bookkeepers won't refer to 'rule 1' or 'rule 2' in daily work, as this particular way of thinking about it has been put together for this study guide, but it may be helpful to think of double-entry in this way at the beginning.

Rule 1 – Bank and Cash

This first rule applies when dealing with bank payments/receipts or cash payments/receipts, and only applies to accounts that can be considered as bank accounts.

Money In =	**Money Out** =
Debit	Credit

Money being paid into the bank would be recorded on the **debit** side of the Bank Account, money being paid out of the bank would be recorded on the **credit** side of the Bank Account.

This rule would also apply equally to the Cash Book, or Cash Account or the Petty Cash Book or Petty Cash Account, or any account involving money transactions, e.g., a Bank Deposit Account. It would not apply to a Bank Loan Account, which would be considered as a liability account.

An example of this can be seen here, where capital (money introduced to the business by the owner) has been paid into the account. This example will be looked at more closely later, with only the debit entry shown here. This is money coming into the business and so is recorded as a debit in the Bank Account. The date format here (01-01) refers to the day and the month, January 1st.

Bank Account (1200)			
Debit *(dr)*	£	Credit *(cr)*	£
01-01 Capital	**20,000**		

Care must be taken to understand that this rule **only** applies to the following accounts:

- Bank Account (or Bank column in the Cash Book - see chapter 5)
- Cash Account (or Cash column in the Cash Book - see chapter 5)
- Petty Cash Account (or Petty Cash Book - see chapter 6)
- Bank Deposit Account

An essential element in understanding double-entry is understanding that every transaction will be both a debit and credit, but in different accounts, as every transaction can be seen as behaving in two different ways simultaneously.

Rule 2 – DEAD CLIC

The second rule of double-entry, which covers all other accounts, is known by many names: DEAD CLIC, DEAP CLIC, or PEARLS, all of which are variations on the same theme. Each will be considered briefly in turn, and students can choose whichever they find most helpful.

There is some controversy over the extent to which these ways of learning double-entry are helpful. They are generally helpful at level 2 when learning the principles of double-entry. However, in the long term it is more helpful to have a deep understanding of how different types of account behave, rather than just memorising methods such as these.

DEAD CLIC

Debits	**Credits**
Expenses will normally have a debit balance but may have some transactions on the credit side.	**L**iabilities will normally have a credit balance but may have some transactions on the debit side.
Assets will normally have a debit balance but may have some transactions on the credit side.	**I**ncome will normally have a credit balance but may have some transactions on the debit side.
Drawings will normally have a debit balance but may have some transactions on the credit side.	**C**apital will normally have a credit balance but may have some transactions on the debit side.

DEAP CLIC

Debits	Credits
Expenses will normally have a debit balance but may have some transactions on the credit side.	**L**iabilities will normally have a credit balance but may have some transactions on the debit side.
Assets will normally have a debit balance but may have some transactions on the credit side.	**I**ncome will normally have a credit balance but may have some transactions on the debit side.
Purchases will normally have a debit balance but may have some transactions on the credit side.	**C**apital will normally have a credit balance but may have some transactions on the debit side.

PEARLS

Purchases will normally have a debit balance, but may have some transactions on the credit side
Expenses will normally have a debit balance, but may have some transactions on the credit side
Assets will normally have a debit balance, but may have some transactions on the credit side
Revenue will normally have a credit balance, but may have some transactions on the debit side
Liabilities will normally have a credit balance, but may have some transactions on the debit side
Sales will normally have a credit balance, but may have some transactions on the debit side

Example 1

The business makes a payment of rent of £1,200, the double-entry for this will be:

Account	Amount	Debit	Credit
Rent Paid	£1,200	✓	
Bank	£1,200		✓

Example 2

The business makes sales of £1,000, the double-entry for this will be:

Account	Amount	Debit	Credit
Bank	£1,000	✓	
Sales	£1,000		✓

Please note that these transactions are not part of the case study.

In each case, the Bank Account follows rule 1, relevant for bank and cash accounts, whereas the Rent Paid Account (expense) and the Sales Account (income, or sales) follow the second rule, as befitting their account type.

Understanding double-entry bookkeeping includes understanding how the two rules work together in a complimentary manner. Not all double-entry transactions will involve the bank, as will be seen in later chapters, in which case each account will follow the rules as consistently befitting its account type.

Opening Entries

Delta Q Bikes Ltd begins trading on January 1st and has several transactions that take place on that day:

"It's my first day of business and I want to get my bookkeeping off to the best start possible by entering all the transactions into the accounts. I know that these opening transactions are traditionally entered as journal entries within the double-entry bookkeeping system. The journal is a book of prime entry used to record double-entry transactions in particular circumstances, such as opening entries for a new business."

Date	Money in	Money out
Jan 1st	**£20,000** paid in by Morgan. This is known as **capital** as it is money introduced by the owner.	
Jan 1st	**£25,000** paid in because of a loan from the bank. This is a **liability** as it is owed back to the bank.	
Jan 1st		**£15,000*** spent on machinery with which to make bikes. This machinery is an **asset** as it has value to the business.
Jan 1st		**£13,500*** spent on raw materials for making the bikes. These are known as **purchases**.

**These figures include VAT at 20%.*

In manual bookkeeping, these opening entries will often be entered in a special part of the bookkeeping system called the **journal**, which is studied in the second unit, Principles of Bookkeeping Controls. In computerised bookkeeping, these are often entered in a part of the software set aside for opening balances.

It is also likely that when setting up accounting software, it will be necessary to enter the basic details of the company before entering any transactions.

Each of these transactions will be looked at in turn, but as they all involve money either coming in or out of the bank, it is helpful first to consider the Bank Account and its role in double-entry bookkeeping.

The Bank Account

The General Ledger (sometimes known as the Nominal Ledger) consists of a number of different accounts that cover the transactions covering the whole range of assets, liabilities, income, expenses, purchases, capital and drawings for a business.

This means that a business is likely to have a General Ledger account called the Bank Account. It may instead, as we shall look at in chapter 5, have a Cash Book, which is used to record both cash and bank transactions, but as it is often easier when first learning double-entry to consider the Bank Account as a separate account.

The Bank Account in the General Ledger is a record of all transactions regarding the bank account of the business, that records in the double-entry bookkeeping system all sums of money either received into or paid from the bank account.

References to Bank Account with capitalisation in this text refers to the Bank Account in the General Ledger of the business bookkeeping system.

As with all accounts in the double-entry bookkeeping system, it is laid out on two sides *(debit and credit),* often known as a 'T' account.

Bank Account (1200)			
Debit *(dr)*	£	Credit *(cr)*	£

The exact layout will vary, and it may look differently in computerised accounting systems, but all the basic principles of a double-entry account are:

- Each account will have both a debit side and a credit side.
- Each transaction will have a debit entry in one account and a credit entry in another.
- The balance of the account is the difference between the sum of the debit entries and the sum of the credit entries within that account, with the balance being shown on the higher side.
- Most accounts will usually have a balance on a particular side (according to double-entry rules), but some accounts can have a balance on either side, examples of which will be seen later.

The Bank Account

Money paid into the Bank Account in the General Ledger will be recorded on the debit side of the account.

Money paid out of the Bank Account in the General Ledger will be recorded on the credit side of the account.

This is opposite to what most people would expect having looked at their bank statements. This is because the bank statement is from the bank's perspective. An asset to the business (money in the bank) is a liability to the bank (money owed by the bank to the business).

This can be seen in practice, in the first of the opening entries for the business.

Transaction 1: £20,000 of Capital paid into the bank.

The very first transaction in the business is for Morgan to pay £20,000 into the bank. In the Bank Account, this will look something like this:

Bank Account (1200)			
Debit *(dr)*	£	Credit *(cr)*	£
01-01 Capital	**20,000**		

New transactions throughout this case study will be highlighted in bold. This is purely for learning purposes and not part of accounting convention.

After this half of the transaction has been made: (it is not yet complete)

- There are debit entries for £20,000 and no credit entries.
- The balance of the account is the difference between the two sides.
- The balance of the account is £20,000.
- This is a debit balance (the higher side).

Note that what is recorded here is:

- The date of the transaction.
- What the transaction is for (Capital – this also serves another purpose).
- The amount (the £ symbol is not required as it is in the heading above).

Double-entry bookkeeping requires two transactions (one debit, one credit). The other half of the transaction is:

Capital Account (3000)			
Debit *(dr)*	£	Credit *(cr)*	£
		01-01 Bank	**20,000**

The Capital Account in the General Ledger records capital put in by the owner*(s)* of a business. Capital is owed back to the owners at some point in the future, as it is their money, and behaves like a liability.

Capital and liability accounts normally have credit entries (although in some cases they may have debit entries) and a credit balance.

Note that what is recorded here is:

- The date of the transaction.
- The other half of the double-entry transaction (Bank).
- The amount (the £ symbol is not required as it is in the heading above).

It is usual in manual double-entry transactions that the details section contains the name of the other double-entry account involved in the transaction. This is why the details in the Bank Account say Capital, and the details in the Capital Account say Bank. This method makes it easy and quick to find the other half of a double-entry transaction.

Coding

Some businesses or software may use different coding conventions, and they are free to do so, but the ranges given below are in regular use throughout the world. Such coding conventions help with consistency within and between businesses, and aid in the preparation of financial statements.

Note that both accounts looked at so far – the Bank Account (1200) and the Capital Account (3000) - have been assigned a number. It is not necessary in bookkeeping that those accounts are exactly that number, but there are common conventions in accounting regarding the numbering of accounts within the General Ledger. For example, accounts involving capital or equity are often in the 3000-3999 range, so it would be just as acceptable for the account code for the Capital Account to be 3010 as 3000. Common coding conventions include:

Common Coding Conventions	
0000-0999	Fixed (non-current) assets
1000-1999	Current assets
2000-2999	Current & non-current liabilities
3000-3999	Capital & equity
4000-4999	Sales
5000-5999	Purchases
6000-7999*	Expenditure
8000-9999	Various

**6000-6999 is often used for sales-related expenses, 7000-7999 is often used for general expenses, but some businesses may use the 8000 range for some expenses.*

Current & Non-Current Assets & Liabilities
Current assets and liabilities are usually those that are short-term, often meaning less than a year. Examples include bank and cash balances, money owed by credit customers or to credit suppliers. Non-current assets and liabilities are usually those that are longer term, often over a year. Examples include loans and mortgages.

Transaction 2: £25,000 paid into the bank from a bank loan.

The second transaction is a bank loan, Morgan has applied for a bank loan under the name of the business, and this has been granted by the bank and paid into the business bank account.

In the Bank Account in the General Ledger, the transaction will look like this:

Bank Account (1200)					
Debit *(dr)*		£	Credit *(cr)*		£
01-01	Capital	20,000			
01-01	**Bank Loan**	**25,000**			

Note the presence of the earlier transaction of capital. As with the injection of capital, the paying into the bank of the bank loan involves money coming into the bank account and is therefore recorded there as a debit. However, the business now also owes money to the bank, a liability.

In the Bank Loan Account the transaction will look like this:

Bank Loan Account (2500)					
Debit *(dr)*		£	Credit *(cr)*		£
			01-01	**Bank**	**25,000**

As with the earlier transaction, the details are that of the other account.

A bank loan is a liability, which although it provides money to the business in the short-term, is eventually owed back to the bank. When payments are made on the loan, these would be debit entries in the Bank Loan Account and credit entries in the Bank Account. As the Bank Loan Account is a liability account, it has been assigned a number that is within the range of liability accounts indicated earlier.

Liabilities
A liability is an amount of money that the business owes to a third party. This could be a loan or an amount owed to a supplier after buying goods on credit. It could also be: • The balance of the Bank Account if it is overdrawn. • The balance of the VAT Account if VAT is owed to HMRC. • The balance of a credit card that has not yet been paid. • Wages yet to be paid to employees, or other payroll-related liabilities (pension fund or trades union contributions, income tax/National Insurance owed to HMRC).

Transaction 3: £15,000 (including VAT) spent on machinery

Now that the business has some money in the bank, it is time to spend some of that money. Firstly, the business buys £15,000 of specialist machinery (including VAT) with which to begin making their bikes, with the double-entry looking like this:

Bank Account (1200)					
Debit *(dr)*		£	Credit *(cr)*		£
01-01	Capital	20,000	**01-01**	**Machinery**	**15,000**
01-01	Bank Loan	25,000			

This is not a credit purchase, in that money changes hands when the purchase takes place.

Machinery Account (0010)					
Debit *(dr)*		£	Credit *(cr)*		£
01-01	**Bank**	**12,500**			

Here, the net value of the machinery is recorded in the Machinery (asset) Account, and the VAT will be recorded in the VAT Account. If the business was not registered for VAT, the whole amount would be recorded in the Machinery Account, which is considered more at level 3.

VAT Account (2200)			
Debit *(dr)*	£	Credit *(cr)*	£
01-01 Bank	**2,500**		

There are some important points to note here:

- **Net** is the amount paid excluding VAT.
- **VAT** is the amount which can be reclaimed from HMRC, as this is a purchase. This VAT is calculated at 20% of the net (or 1/6 of the gross) throughout level 2.
- **Gross** is the total amount, and is recorded in the Bank Account, as the actual amount of money that owed/owing.

This is the first example that you have seen of a double-entry transaction that is more than two entries, in this case, two debits and one credit.

Account	Amount	Debit	Credit
VAT	£2,500	✓	
Machinery	£12,500	✓	
Bank	£15,000		✓

However, it illustrates an important principle: **in any double-entry transaction, the sum of the credits should always equal the sum of the debits.**

In this case, the Bank Account entry is a credit entry as money is being paid out of the account. The debit entry is in the Machinery Account, as this is an asset account.

VAT is recorded in a separate account as VAT-registered businesses must record the VAT on all transactions, whether output tax (VAT on sales) or input tax (VAT on purchases). VAT-registered businesses will have one or more VAT accounts that will enable them to do this.

This means that when businesses come to complete and submit their VAT return, usually but not always four times a year, as the information has been accurately recorded, the VAT Return can be calculated efficiently, and any payments made or sums reclaimed.

The VAT Account will have a debit balance (an asset) if you are owed money by HMRC or a credit balance (a liability) if you owe money to HMRC.

Assets

Assets are an item that is owned by the business and has material value, or money owed to the business by a customer who has bought goods on credit.

It could also be:

- The balance of the Bank Account if there is money in the bank.
- The balance of the VAT Account if money is owed by HMRC (a debit balance).
- Any cash held by the business (for example, petty cash, or the balance of the Cash column in the Cash Book).

It is usually relatively straightforward to decide whether something a business owns should be viewed as an asset, as it is usually something that has value and could be used, if necessary, to meet debts and other commitments. For example, a company vehicle could be sold to pay a debt, whereas that would not be true for a box of paper clips.

VAT Calculations

Many of the calculations in this unit will involve sums that are either inclusive or exclusive of VAT, the latter sometimes being referred to as net of VAT.

Including VAT = VAT at 20% has already been included in this figure:
Example: £120.00 including VAT (£100 net + £20 VAT)
To determine how much VAT has been added to a VAT-inclusive figure, divide by 6, e.g., £120 / 6 = £20. This is also known as the VAT fraction.

Excluding VAT = VAT at 20% has NOT already been included in this figure:
Example £100.00 excluding VAT (£100 net but £20 VAT has not yet been added)
To determine how much VAT to add to a net figure, divide by 5, e.g., £100 / 5 = £20.

There are also other ways of performing VAT calculations. It is not essential to use the method above if you have a technique that works just as well.

On rare occasions, different methods of calculating VAT will result in different final numbers, depending on whether the VAT or the net is rounded first. However, this is not likely to happen in any calculations for your AAT exams. In these cases, ensure that the gross total is correct, even if the net or VAT are different by £0.01 from other calculation methods, as this is considered acceptable in real-world calculations.

Transaction 4: £13,500 (including VAT) spent on raw materials

Finally, on the first day of trading, the business has spent £13,500 on raw materials that will become part of the completed bikes once the machinery is up and running. As with the purchase of machinery, VAT must be accounted for in this transaction.

Bank Account (1200)					
Debit *(dr)*		£	Credit *(cr)*		£
01-01	Capital	20,000	01-01	Machinery	15,000
01-01	Bank Loan	25,000	**01-01**	**Purchases**	**13,500**

Purchases (5000)					
Debit *(dr)*		£	Credit *(cr)*		£
01-01	**Bank**	**11,250**			

Here, the net value of the raw materials is recorded in the Purchases Account, and the VAT will be recorded in the VAT Account.

VAT Account (2200)					
Debit *(dr)*		£	Credit *(cr)*		£
01-01	Bank	2,500			
01-01	**Bank**	**2,250**			

The Purchases Account has been given a code of 5000 to reflect its status as a purchases account within the General Ledger. This is a cash purchase, in that money has been paid at the time of purchase. The supplier is likely to have provided an invoice with the goods. Invoices and other documents will be examined in chapter 3.

The Accounting Equation

There are various means by which an accountant or bookkeeper can use information from the accounts of the business to either gauge the business's health or to draw conclusions regarding the business.

If it is desirable to calculate the amount of capital within the business, one of these is known as the **accounting equation**. The accounting equation calculates the amount of capital in the business by comparing it to the amount of assets and liabilities.

The formula is:

Assets – Liabilities = Capital

This formula is also the basis of the **Statement of Financial Position** that many businesses must produce yearly as part of their required financial statements.

The Statement of Financial Position lists the assets and liabilities of a business at a given time, usually the end of the financial year, and therefore can be used to determine how much capital is in the business. It is a requirement of limited companies and some partnerships. The statement can be used by shareholders and anyone interested in the financial health of the business, such as the business owner or someone looking to invest in the business.

The other formula generally required by businesses is the **Statement of Profit or Loss**. The formula is:

Income – Expenses = Profit

(or loss if the answer is a negative figure)

The Statement of Profit or Loss shows the income and expenses of a business over a 12-month period, to determine whether the business is making a profit or loss, and is a requirement of limited companies and some partnerships. The statement can be used by shareholders and anyone who is interested in the financial health of the business, such as the business owner or someone looking to invest in the business.

Financial statements are studied in detail at both level 3 and level 4.

Modern accounting software can easily generate the Statement of Financial Position and the Statement of Profit or Loss. This means that it is easier than in manual bookkeeping to determine the health or profit-making status of a business at any given time than in the past.

Students working through this scenario in accounting software could prove this by generating a Statement of Financial Position and Statement of Profit or Loss at the end of each chapter to see how the business is performing at any given moment.

The accounting equation can be applied to Delta Q Bikes Ltd to determine the amount of capital in the business at the end of the first day of trading.

Assets	**Total: £45,000**
	£16,500 (Bank Account balance) £12,500 (Machinery Account balance) £4,750 (VAT Account balance) £11,250 (Purchases Account balance)
minus **Liabilities**	**Total: £25,000**
	£25,000 (Bank Loan Account balance)
equals **Capital**	**Total: £20,000** (Capital Account balance)

VAT here is an asset as it is a debit balance reflecting money spent on purchases that can be reclaimed from HMRC. If the balance of the VAT were a credit balance it would be a liability.

The raw materials purchased are considered as inventory or stock, and inventory is an asset. This is the major difference between purchases and expenses, the latter of which are the running costs of the business and do not generally contain any asset value.

The relationship between assets and liabilities keeps the accounting equation balanced.

For example:

- The purchase of a computer for £1,000 would reduce the asset of the Bank Account by £1,000 whilst increasing the asset of the Computer at Cost Account by £1,000, ensuring capital remains the same.
- The receipt of a bank loan of £5,000 would increase the asset of the Bank Account by £5,000 whilst increasing the liability of the Bank Loan Account by £5,000, ensuring capital remains the same.

Balancing Accounts

In manual bookkeeping, it is essential to balance accounts. How often this is done will vary on the needs of the business. All accounts will be balanced at least once a year at the end of the financial year. Many accounts will be balanced either monthly or weekly as appropriate.

In this case study, some accounts will be balanced monthly, to show the process at work. Although Morgan may not need to balance any of the business' accounts at this time, it will be useful to look at one of the accounts and balance it to get understanding of the process.

The account used to show this will be the Bank Account, as this is currently the account with the most transactions:

Bank Account (1200)					
Debit *(dr)*		£	Credit *(cr)*		£
01-01	Capital	20,000	01-01	Machinery	15,000
01-01	Bank Loan	25,000	01-01	Raw Materials	13,500

Balancing a bookkeeping account manually has various steps:

1. Add up each side of the account (debit and credit).
2. Create a transaction on the smaller side numerically (this is called the balance carried down).
3. Total both sides, which should now be the same amount.
4. Create a transaction on the side which was larger numerically (this is called the balance brought down).

Each of these steps can be seen in turn:

Step 1: Add up each side of the account

Bank Account (1200)					
Debit *(dr)*		£	Credit *(cr)*		£
01-01	Capital	20,000	01-01	Machinery	15,000
01-01	Bank Loan	25,000	01-01	Raw Materials	13,500

The sum of the debit side is £45,000, the sum of the credit side £28,500.

The difference between the two sides (£45,000 - £28,500 = £16,500) must then be entered into the Bank Account:

Step 2: Enter the balance carried down

Bank Account (1200)					
Debit *(dr)*		£	Credit *(cr)*		£
01-01	Capital	20,000	01-01	Machinery	15,000
01-01	Bank Loan	25,000	01-01	Raw Materials	13,500
			01-01	**Balance c/d**	**16,500**

The balance carried *down* (abbreviated as the balance c/d) is always dated on the last date of the period in question, in this case, January 1st, or it could be the last day of the week or of the month, as appropriate.

The two sides of the account are then calculated again, and they should be identical.

Step 3: Add the new totals for both sides of the account

Bank Account (1200)					
Debit *(dr)*		£	Credit *(cr)*		£
01-01	Capital	20,000	01-01	Machinery	15,000
01-01	Bank Loan	25,000	01-01	Raw Materials	13,500
			01-01	Balance c/d	16,500
	Total	**45,000**	Total		**45,000**

It is worth noting that the totals will always be the sum of the higher side, in this case £45,000, and that the balance c/d is the transaction that makes the two sides balance, hence balancing the account.

The balance c/d is not the true balance of the account, because it is on the wrong side, as that is added in the final step.

Step 4: Add the balance brought down

Bank Account (1200)					
Debit *(dr)*		£	Credit *(cr)*		£
01-01	Capital	20,000	01-01	Machinery	15,000
01-01	Bank Loan	25,000	01-01	Raw Materials	13,500
			01-01	Balance c/d	16,500
	Total	**45,000**	Total		**45,000**
02-01	**Balance b/d**	**16,500**			

The fact that the balance is brought down on the debit side is an indicator that the account has a debit balance. As the Bank Account records the balance as an asset (if the business has money) or a liability (if the business is overdrawn), a debit balance in the account indicates that the business has £16,500 in the bank.

As the balance c/d is usually dated on the last day of a time period, the balance b/d is usually dated on the first day of the next time period, as demonstrated in this example.

If an account does not have transactions on one side, which is typical for many expense and income accounts, the principles are the same. In this case, the difference between the two sides will still form the basis of the calculation of the balance.

For example, an account has transactions on the debit side of £4000, but no transactions on the credit side. In this case, the difference between the two sides will be £4000.

It may also be the case that an account has an opening balance at the beginning of a time period. This will be indicated by either a balance b/d or it is sometimes shown as a balance b/f (balance brought forward). Either is acceptable, and in exam situations you may see both in use.

Computerised accounting automatically balances accounts as transactions are added. However, students will be expected to know and demonstrate the knowledge of how to balance accounts manually at both level 2 and level 3.

Note that the balancing here is only an example, and the Bank Account will be seen balanced again as part of the case study, with a different date, in the next chapter.

Account Balances

At the end of every chapter, we will look at the balances of the accounts so far. This will be shown in the **trial balance** format, which will be considered in more detail in the Principles of Bookkeeping Controls unit.

This will be helpful to see what account balances have changed during the chapter, as well as the relationship between debits and credits.

A correct trial balance will mean that the sum of the accounts with debit balances will equal the sum of the accounts with credit balances. Students who are entering the transactions into accounting software will be able to generate their own trial balance to check for accuracy, although different software may list them in a different order.

The purpose of the trial balance is a check on the arithmetical bookkeeping and as a way of finding and eliminating errors. Although a careful reading of a trial balance can give some indication as to the state of a business, that is not its primary purpose.

By examining the trial balance as it develops over the coming chapters, students will come to understand its purpose more, and gain experience in learning which accounts have debit or credit balances.

Note that previously, transactions and balances have been listed to the nearest £ (although the nearest pence is implied), whereas in future transactions and balances they will be recorded to the nearest pence, which is two decimal places.

Trial Balance Delta Q Bikes Ltd January 1st			
Nominal Code	**Account**	**Debit £**	**Credit £**
0010	Machinery	12,500.00	
1200	Bank	16,500.00	
2200	VAT	4,750.00	
2500	Bank Loan		25,000.00
3000	Capital		20,000.00
5000	Purchases	11,250.00	
	Total	**45,000.00**	**45,000.00**

Digital Focus

Students should practice the following skills in computerised accounting software.

1. Setting up a company.
2. Entering the opening balances to individual accounts as per the examples in this chapter.
3. Entering the transactions listed in the chapter.

The following information can be used in setting up the fictional company*: (if required by software)*

Name: Morgan Rothby
Company Name: Delta Q Bikes Ltd
Unit 3b
Ashwell Business Park
Ashwell
AS17 4BX
VAT no: 798204391

Some accounting software may also request a telephone number, in which case, try to input a telephone number that is not genuine if using cloud-based software.

Entering opening transactions may involve finding and renaming the relevant accounts in the General Ledger (which may be referred to as the Nominal Ledger). A best-fit approach is usually acceptable, within the context of the numerical ranges expressed earlier in the chapter.

Traditionally, opening balances are entered as journal entries, and so students should be encouraged to enter opening balances using the journal, rather than as bank payments or receipts.

Along with those skills, they could also practice the following to see the impact of those exercises.

4. Finding and examining an Audit Trail to see the double-entry transactions that they have made.
5. Finding and examining a Trial Balance to see the balances of the accounts after entering the opening transactions and balances.

Summary

Most bookkeeping follows the double-entry principle.

In double-entry bookkeeping every entry is recorded twice – once as a debit entry in one account, and once as a credit entry in another account. The accounts in which the transactions take place are related to the nature of the transaction.

Some transactions will have three entries. The most common example of this is when entries involve a VAT-registered business needing to make a third entry in which to record the VAT either collected and owed to HMRC or paid and reclaimable from HMRC.

Opening entries for a new business will usually involve entries in a book of prime entry called the Journal, which in computerised accounting automatically enters the required double-entry. In manual bookkeeping, the double-entry will need to be done manually.

Bank & Cash accounts will involve debit entries when the value of those amounts is increasing (e.g., a receipt) and credit entries when the value of those accounts is decreasing (e.g., a payment).

This is the opposite of what can be seen in a statement received from the bank, because the statement received from a bank is from the bank's perspective.

Most accounts will always have a debit balance or always have a credit balance.

Some accounts, most notably the Bank Account and the VAT Account, can have either a debit or a credit balance.

The Bank Account will have a debit balance if there is money in the bank, and a credit balance if the account is overdrawn.

The VAT Account will have a debit balance if money is owed from HMRC, and a credit balance if money is owed to HMRC.

Although computerised accounting software will automatically balance accounts, there is a manual method of balancing accounts of which students need to be aware, in particular the behaviour of the totals, the balance c/d (carried down) and the balance b/d (brought down) which is sometimes referred to as the balance b/f (brought forward) at the beginning of a time period.

The Accounting Equation can explain the relationship between assets, liabilities and capital: assets – liabilities = capital.

Skills & Knowledge Test – Chapter 2

QUESTION 5

For each of the following accounts, identify the account type.

	Asset	Liability	Income	Expense	Purchase	Capital
Money in the bank						
Bank overdrawn						
VAT owed by HMRC						
VAT owed to HMRC						
Money from sales						
Buying raw materials						
Rent paid						
Rent received						
Money paid in by owner						
Insurance payment						
Computer equipment						
Bank loan						

QUESTION 6

For each of the accounts below, select whether it would normally have a debit or credit balance.

	Debit	Credit
Money in the bank		
Bank overdrawn		
VAT owed by HMRC		
VAT owed to HMRC		
Sales		
Purchases		
Rent paid		
Rent received		
Capital		
Insurance		
Computer Equipment		
Bank Loan		

QUESTION 7

Enter the following transaction into the double-entry records. The business has made a payment to the insurance company of £300. There is no VAT to consider.

Account	Amount £	Debit	Credit

QUESTION 8

Enter the following transaction into the double-entry records. The business owner has made drawings of £1000 from the bank.

Account	Amount £	Debit	Credit

QUESTION 9

Enter the following transaction into the double-entry records. The business has taken out a bank loan of £18,500.

Account	Amount £	Debit	Credit

QUESTION 10

Enter the following transaction into the double-entry records. The business has made a cash purchase of raw materials for £250 plus VAT.

Account	Amount £	Debit	Credit

QUESTION 11

For the following calculations of the accounting formula, assets minus liabilities equals capital, complete the table by filling in the blanks.

Assets	Liabilities	Capital
25,000		12,250
	48,673	91,572
32,800	9,750	
82,855		41,000
	4,300	11,972
108,465	23,911	

QUESTION 12

A business takes out a bank loan of £5,000. Which of the following will occur?

Assets will increase, liabilities will remain the same	
Liabilities will increase, assets will remain the same	
Assets will increase, liabilities will increase	

QUESTION 13

Identify whether each of the following transactions will be a credit or a debit in the Bank Account in the General Ledger.

	Debit	Credit
Payment of wages to employees		
Payment of insurance premium		
Receipt of money from sales		
Money paid in by the owner		
Money drawn out by the owner		
Payment of VAT bill to HMRC		
Receipt of VAT refund from HMRC		
Payment of rent		
Bank loan received		

QUESTION 14

Balance the following Receivables Ledger Control Account. *Note, you may have not seen this account yet, but this activity will still help you with your balancing skills, as well as introducing an account you will see in a subsequent chapter. The principles of balancing are identical to the examples seen in this chapter.*

Receivables Ledger Control Account					
Debit *(dr)*		£	Credit *(cr)*		£
02-01	Credit Sales	12,573	08-01	Money received	4.911
	Total		**Total**		

QUESTION 15

Balance the following Payables Ledger Control Account. *Note, you may have not seen this account yet, but this activity will still help you with your balancing skills, as well as introducing an account you will see in a subsequent chapter. The principles of balancing are exactly the same as examples seen in this chapter.*

Payables Ledger Control Account					
Debit *(dr)*		£	Credit *(cr)*		£
14-01	Money Paid	11,100	08-01	Credit Purchases	21.284
15-01	Discounts received	969			
	Total		**Total**		

QUESTION 16

Balance the following Wages Account.

Wages Account					
Debit *(dr)*		£	Credit *(cr)*		£
03-01	Wages	500			
10-01	Wages	500			
17-01	Wages	500			
	Total			**Total**	

QUESTION 17

Balance the following Bank Account. *Note, this account is a little different, as it has an opening balance (b/f). It should be treated exactly as any other transaction and counted.*

Bank Account					
Debit *(dr)*		£	Credit *(cr)*		£
03-01	Balance b/f	2500	03-01	Wages	500
04-01	Capital	1211	09-01	Insurance	850
11-01	Sales	850	19-01	Wages	500
	Total			**Total**	

This section has been created for you should you wish to use it to make notes or for calculations.

Credit Purchases

Introduction

Businesses use documents to facilitate the process of sales and purchases. These documents provide an important paper trail that can help resolve problems that may occur between the buyer (customer) and the seller (supplier) of goods and services.

Many of these documents are nowadays created and sent electronically (either by email or downloadable from a website) rather than on paper. Some documents are also in less common use than in the past. Bookkeepers need to be aware of and be able to create and interpret these documents as well as understanding their role in the buying & selling process.

The key sales & purchases documents are:

Document Types	
Price Quotation	A document provided by the seller of goods and services, outlining the price the buyer will pay should they place an order.
Purchase Order	A document provided by the buyer of goods and services, outlining to the seller the goods and services that they wish to buy.
Invoice	The key document provided by the seller, outlining the items sold, the cost of those items, and when/how the buyer should pay.
Goods Received Note	A document completed by the buyer, which acknowledges receipt of the goods purchased.
Credit Note	A document provided by the seller to the buyer when goods or services are returned or are incomplete and reduces the value of the invoice to which it relates.
Statement of Account	A document sent by the seller to the buyer outlining the balance of the account, and any related transactions.

Later in the chapter, we will also look at the role of the Remittance Advice.

The exact layout of these documents will vary from business to business. The style of the documents in this book is one of many potential options. Many of these documents (for example, purchase orders, invoices & credit notes) can be generated automatically by computerised accounting software with customisable templates.

Before examining each of these in detail, let us remind ourselves of the scenario for this unit.

Scenario
Morgan has started a business making and selling bicycles. This business is called Delta Q Bikes Ltd and makes both standard and electric bicycles. Bicycles are sold to shops, who then sell them on to customers, and are also sold direct to customers by Delta Q Bikes Ltd via their online shop and website. Morgan has put some of her own money into the business (this is known as capital) as well as money from a friend and a bank loan (which are known as liabilities). She has rented a property from which to manufacture bikes and store them in a warehouse and has hired two other employees. Morgan has also invested in specialist machinery (an asset) for manufacturing the bikes. The business will use a double-entry bookkeeping system, which uses a series of day books (for credit sales and purchases) linked to a Receivables Ledger, a Payables Ledger, and the General Ledger. The business will buy components and other items from suppliers, which are known as credit purchases, and will sell finished goods to shops, which are known as credit sales. Cash sales to retail customers, from the online website, are also recorded. A cash book and petty cash book are used, both of which are books of prime entry and double-entry, and will record the money element of all purchases, expenses and income, as well as any drawings made by the owner.

Morgan will buy several items on credit from suppliers (these are known as credit purchases) as well as selling on credit to customers (these are known as credit sales).

This chapter will consider credit purchases, looking at purchase documents from the perspective of Delta Q Bikes Ltd as the business buys from suppliers on credit.

Students should be aware that if they are practising entering transactions into accounting software, the software will do the entries into the Payables Ledger Control Account (which may go by another name) automatically, so students should not usually attempt to enter them into that account.

Price Quotation

> A document provided by the seller of goods and services, outlining the price the buyer will pay should they place an order.

Delta Q Bikes Ltd has requested a price from FabFrames Ltd, a producer of bike frames for traditional and electric bicycles. Although in this scenario the price quotation is provided by a formal document, it may also be provided in the style of a price quoted on a webpage, or in an email or telephone call. However, the key components are likely to be the same.

2021 and 2022 are the years used in this scenario, although students are free to use suitable years of their choice when entering transactions in accounting software.

Price Quotation	
From: FabFrames Ltd 25 Meadowcroft Estate Ashwell AS19 2HF VAT No: 145853235	**To:** Delta Q Bikes Ltd Unit 3b Ashwell Business Park Ashwell AS17 4BX VAT No: 798204391
Item(s) & Price: 10 x Electric Blue bicycle frame, £90.00 excluding VAT.	
Signed: *C Chambers*	**Date:** 28/12/2021

Other details may be included, such as the seller's telephone number or email address. Prices are often listed, excluding VAT.

Most businesses will have the codes, information and costs of products available in a price list, either paper-based (e.g., catalogue), or digital (e.g., website).

Purchase Order

> A document provided by the buyer of goods and services, outlining to the seller the goods and services that they wish to buy.

Purchase Order

From:	**To:**
Delta Q Bikes Ltd Unit 3b Ashwell Business Park Ashwell AS17 4BX VAT No: 798204391	FabFrames Ltd 25 Meadowcroft Estate Ashwell AS19 2HF VAT No: 145853235
Purchase Order No: PO452	**Date:** 30/12/2021

Product Code	Quantity	Description
EBFM	10	Electric Blue bicycle frame

Authorised:	**Date:**
S Kenworthy	30/12/2021

Purchase orders may or may not contain the price of the item, either is quite common. The price is not necessary on a purchase order if a price quotation has been given previously, as it is presumed that the price given in the price quotation is to be applied to the purchase order if no significant period of time has passed.

EBFM is a recognisable product code, to ensure that the correct item is ordered.

Invoice

The key document provided by the seller, outlining the items sold, the cost of those items, and when/how the buyer should pay.

<table>
<tr><td colspan="8">Invoice</td></tr>
<tr><td colspan="4">From:

FabFrames Ltd
25 Meadowcroft Estate
Ashwell
AS19 2HF

VAT No: 145853235</td><td colspan="4">To:

Delta Q Bikes Ltd
Unit 3b
Ashwell Business Park
Ashwell
AS17 4BX

VAT No: 798204391</td></tr>
<tr><td colspan="2">Invoice no:</td><td colspan="2">Account</td><td colspan="2">Your reference:</td><td colspan="2">Date:</td></tr>
<tr><td colspan="2">FF431</td><td colspan="2">DEL001</td><td colspan="2">PO452</td><td colspan="2">01/01/2022</td></tr>
<tr><td>Product Code</td><td>Description</td><td>Quantity</td><td>Price £</td><td>Unit</td><td>Total £</td><td>Discount %</td><td>Net £</td></tr>
<tr><td>EBFM</td><td>Electric Blue Frame</td><td>10</td><td>90.00</td><td>each</td><td>900.00</td><td>0.00</td><td>900.00</td></tr>
<tr><td colspan="5" rowspan="3">Terms: 60 days
Carriage paid
E&OE</td><td>Goods Total</td><td colspan="2">£900.00</td></tr>
<tr><td>VAT</td><td colspan="2">£180.00</td></tr>
<tr><td>Total</td><td colspan="2">£1080.00</td></tr>
</table>

An invoice may also include information from the seller to the buyer on how they can pay the invoice, for example, the seller's bank details, although this is not required. Many invoices nowadays can be produced automatically by accounting software, and even emailed to the client directly from the software.

Goods Received Note

A document completed by the buyer, which acknowledges receipt of the goods purchased. This may be provided by the seller or the buyer.

<table>
<tr><th colspan="3">Goods Received</th></tr>
<tr><td colspan="2">From:

FabFrames Ltd
25 Meadowcroft Estate
Ashwell
AS19 2HF

VAT No: 145853235</td><td>To:

Delta Q Bikes Ltd
Unit 3b
Ashwell Business Park
Ashwell
AS17 4BX

VAT No: 798204391</td></tr>
<tr><td>Goods received note no:</td><td>Your reference</td><td>Date:</td></tr>
<tr><td>FFGR198</td><td>PO452</td><td>02/01/2022</td></tr>
<tr><td>Product Code</td><td>Quantity</td><td>Description</td></tr>
<tr><td>EBFM</td><td>10</td><td>Electric Blue Frame</td></tr>
<tr><td colspan="2">Received by:</td><td>Date:</td></tr>
<tr><td colspan="2">S Kenworthy
One bike frame damaged</td><td>02/01/2022</td></tr>
</table>

A Goods Received Note may be completed by the buyer on receipt of the goods to acknowledge the quality and quantity of goods received as correct or incorrect. This Goods Received note acknowledges that one bike frame is damaged.

Credit Note

> A document provided by the seller to the buyer when goods or services are returned or are incomplete and reduces the value of the invoice to which it relates.

Credit Note							
From: FabFrames Ltd 25 Meadowcroft Estate Ashwell AS19 2HF VAT No: 145853235				**To:** Delta Q Bikes Ltd Unit 3b Ashwell Business Park Ashwell AS17 4BX VAT No: 798204391			
Credit note no: CRN215				**Reason for credit:** 1 frame damaged			
Invoice no:		**Account**		**Your reference:**		**Date:**	
FF431		DEL001		PO452		03/01/2022	
Product Code	**Description**	**Quantity**	**Price**	**Unit**	**Total**	**Discount %**	**Net**
EBFM	Electric blue frame	1	90.00	each	90.00	0.00	90.00
					Goods Total	90.00	
					VAT	18.00	
					Total	108.00	

A credit note looks very similar to an invoice, and is often linked to a particular invoice, as in this case. Credit notes can be issued for other reasons, such as discounts, as shall be seen later. Although in an actual transaction, FabFrames Ltd may have sent a bicycle frame to replace the one that was damaged, the credit note process for a return here is shown as part of the learning process.

Statement of Account

A document sent by the seller to the buyer outlining the balance of the account, and any related transactions.

Statement of Account				
From: FabFrames Ltd 25 Meadowcroft Estate Ashwell AS19 2HF VAT No: 145853235		**To:** Delta Q Bikes Ltd Unit 3b Ashwell Business Park Ashwell AS17 4BX VAT No: 798204391		
Account: DEL001		**Date:** 31/01/2022		
Date	**Details**	**Debit £**	**Credit £**	**Balance £**
01/01/2022	Balance b/f			0.00
01/01/2022	Invoice FF431	1080.00		1080.00
04/01/2022	Credit note CRN215		108.00	972.00
Payments may be made electronically to FabFrames Ltd Sort code: 01-26-91 Account no: 45813290			**Total:**	£972.00

A statement of account should list all transactions for the time period and provide a suggestion as to means of payment.

Statements of account may be issued according to the wants of the supplier, e.g., weekly or monthly, and can also be issued on demand. In modern accounting, many businesses can often log in to an online account and see their balance with a supplier at any time.

Discounts

Discounts can be offered by a supplier (seller) to a customer (buyer) for one of three reasons:

Discount Types	
Trade Discount	Usually offered to regular customers as a set percentage, as an incentive to keep buying from that supplier.
Bulk Discount	Usually offered when purchases are over a certain level (either in percentage, unit or monetary terms).
Prompt Payment Discount *(PPD)*	An incentive offered to encourage customers to pay earlier than the agreed invoice terms.

Students will be expected to be able to identify the differences between the three types of discount and identify each from a description or financial document such as an invoice.

Discounts that students will identify at this level fall into the following two types:

Calculated on the invoice and forming part of the invoice total:

- Trade Discount
- Bulk Discount

These amounts are discounted from the net amount on the invoice and must be discounted from the net before VAT is added.

Mentioned on the invoice but only calculated if the customer pays within the agreed time limit:

- Prompt Payment Discount

This amount is not calculated on the invoice but will be calculated from the total (gross) amount when the customer pays, presuming that they have met the conditions of the PPD as mentioned in the invoice.

Invoice (with trade or bulk discount)

This invoice shows a discount of 10%, which is discounted from the net, before VAT and the gross total being calculated. Both trade and bulk discounts behave in this manner.

Invoice

From:	**To:**
FabFrames Ltd 25 Meadowcroft Estate Ashwell AS19 2HF VAT No: 145853235	Delta Q Bikes Ltd Unit 3b Ashwell Business Park Ashwell AS17 4BX VAT No: 798204391

Invoice no:	**Account**	**Your reference:**	**Date:**
FF431	DEL001	PO452	01/01/2022

Product Code	**Description**	**Quantity**	**Price £**	**Unit**	**Total £**	**Discount %**	**Net £**
EBFM	Electric Blue Frame	10	90.00	each	900.00	10.00	810.00

Terms: 60 days Carriage paid E&OE	**Goods Total**	£810.00
	VAT	£162.00
	Total	£972.00

Invoice (with prompt payment discount)

This invoice shows a prompt payment discount of 5%, which is not calculated on the invoice.

If Delta Q Bikes Ltd pay the invoice within 7 days, they will:

a) Pay 95% of the gross total of the invoice (invoice amount minus 5% PPD).
b) Receive a credit note from FabStyle for the value of the discount - £54.00 (£45.00 net, £9.00 VAT). Both businesses will enter the credit note into their relevant accounting systems, and the invoice will show as paid.

Later in this chapter, we will see the impact of a credit note for a purchase return and a payment using the PPD (a discount received).

<table>
<tr><td colspan="8">Invoice</td></tr>
<tr><td colspan="4">From:

FabFrames Ltd
25 Meadowcroft Estate
Ashwell
AS19 2HF

VAT No: 145853235</td><td colspan="4">To:

Delta Q Bikes Ltd
Unit 3b
Ashwell Business Park
Ashwell
AS17 4BX

VAT No: 798204391</td></tr>
<tr><td colspan="2">Invoice no:</td><td colspan="2">Account</td><td colspan="2">Your reference:</td><td colspan="2">Date:</td></tr>
<tr><td colspan="2">FF431</td><td colspan="2">DEL001</td><td colspan="2">PO452</td><td colspan="2">01/01/2022</td></tr>
<tr><td>Product Code</td><td>Description</td><td>Quantity</td><td>Price £</td><td>Unit</td><td>Total £</td><td>Discount %</td><td>Net £</td></tr>
<tr><td>EBFM</td><td>Electric Blue Frame</td><td>10</td><td>90.00</td><td>each</td><td>900.00</td><td>0.00</td><td>900.00</td></tr>
<tr><td colspan="5" rowspan="3">Terms: 60 days
Carriage paid
E&OE
PPD - 5% if paid within 7 days of invoice</td><td>Goods Total</td><td colspan="2">£900.00</td></tr>
<tr><td>VAT</td><td colspan="2">£180.00</td></tr>
<tr><td>Total</td><td colspan="2">£1080.00</td></tr>
</table>

Prompt Payment Discount Declaration

When offering a Prompt Payment Discount, the supplier has one of two options:

1. Issue a VAT invoice for the total value of the supply plus VAT, then issue a credit note for the amount of any discount. This is the process that is followed in this chapter.

or

2. Issue an invoice including the terms of the PPD and a statement that the customer can only recover as input tax the VAT actually paid to the supplier.

In this second case, there is wording recommended by HMRC which should also be on the invoice:

"A discount of X% of the full price applies if payment is made within Y days of the invoice date. No credit note will be issued. Following payment, you must ensure you have only recovered the VAT actually paid."

Prompt Payment Discount Checks

Whether a supplier (seller) or buyer (customer), checks should be undertaken to ensure that a PPD has been correctly taken when payments are made or received. Key checks include:

1. Is it stated on the invoice that PPD can be taken? (If not, then no PPD can be taken).
2. If PPD can be taken, has the correct percentage been taken? (And calculated correctly).
3. If PPD can be taken, has it been taken within the relevant period? (Within a certain number of days as stated on the invoice).

Prompt Payment Discount can be an effective method for a business that sells goods and services to encourage customers to play sooner rather than later, encouraging the positive cash flow of the business.

Suppliers will need to be aware of their profit margins on the products that they sell, to use Prompt Payment Discount wisely without negatively impacting the profit of the business.

When taking a Prompt Payment Discount, a check also needs to be made that any discount taken on an invoice also takes into account any relevant credit notes related to it that will further reduce the overall value of the invoice, and therefore affect the amount of the discount.

Coding

Businesses are free to use any coding system they prefer for customer codes, invoicing, purchase orders, credit notes, etc. Sometimes, businesses will inherit codes from the system suggested by their computerised accounting software, although businesses are free to change those codes as best suits their needs.

Coding can be:

Numeric – just numbers, e.g., 123

Alphabetic – just letters, e.g., ABC

Alphanumeric – a combination of numbers and letters, e.g., ABC123

The latter is the most common.

Common coding systems are:

POXXX – purchase orders, where PO stands for purchase order, XXX is a number to indicate which purchase order, e.g., PO123.

INVXXX – invoices, where INV stands for invoice, XXX is a number to indicate which invoice, e.g., INV001.

CNXXX – credit notes, where CN stands for credit notes, XXX is a number to indicate which credit note, e.g., CN456.

Another common coding system you will see in your studies is customer and supplier coding, e.g.

HAR001 – this is a common code for a company called Harper Limited.

HAR002 – this could be used for another company with a similar name, e.g., Harper PLC.

You should be aware that in some computerised accounting systems, once a code has been assigned to a customer or supplier, it may not be possible to change it.

As well as using codes for documents, customers and suppliers, businesses will also use General Ledger codes to analyse purchases. The most common code range used in the General Ledgers for purchases is in the 5000-5999 range.

Morgan has decided that the relevant code for this purchase in the bookkeeping system is to use code 5000 to analyse Purchases. This account was used in the previous chapter for the purchase of raw materials.

Recording Credit Purchases

Businesses that buy on credit need a system of recording the value of purchases. They need to be able to separately record:

- The value of the net purchase.
- The amount of the VAT to be paid to or claimed from HMRC.
- The total amount of the liability owed (for a purchase). This needs to be done both in the General Ledger and the Payables Ledger.

Typically, this is done with a series of day books as follows:

Purchases Day Book (for credit purchases)
Purchases Returns Day Book (for credit purchases returns)
Discounts Received Day Book (to record prompt payment discounts received)

Purchases transactions are initially recorded in the relevant day book (book of prime entry) and then transferred to the correct accounts in the General Ledger.

The day books described above and the transfer processes to the ledger accounts described in the following pages are only for credit purchases. Credit sales, although a very similar process, will be identified later.

Credit purchases = buy now, pay later. An invoice is sent with the goods, and the buyer pays within the prescribed payment period.

Cash purchases = buy now, pay now. The payment takes place at the same time as transfer of ownership of the goods.

The term credit or cash refers to the nature of the transaction (buy now pay later or buy now pay now), not the payment method. The terms cash and credit can have multiple meanings in accountancy and bookkeeping. When transferring transactions involving VAT from purchases-related day books to ledgers, it is always the case that:

- There will be two credits and one debit, or two debits and one credit.
- The sum of the credits will equal to the sum of the debits.
- One account will always be the Payables Ledger Control Account.
- One account will always be the VAT Account.
- The other account will be named after the relevant day book.

Purchases

The following purchases have been recorded in the Purchases Day Book for Delta Q Bikes Ltd.

Purchases Day Book						
Date	**Details**	**Invoice**	**PL Code**	**Net £**	**VAT £**	**Total £**
01-01	FabFrames Ltd	FF431	FAB001	900.00	180.00	1080.00
08-01	WonderWheels	PIN276	WON001	750.00	150.00	900.00
10-01	SuperSuspension	INV561	SUP001	235.00	47.00	282.00
			TOTALS:	1885.00	377.00	262.00

This day book includes the transaction between Delta Q Bikes Ltd and FabFrames Ltd seen earlier in the chapter, as well as two other credit purchases. A column is included here to show each supplier's Payables Ledger account code. If desired, a separate row or section could also include the General Ledger codes for the Net, VAT & Total columns. There could also be separate net columns if there were more than one purchases category. This would then be referred to as an analysed day book. An example will be shown later in this chapter.

For each of these purchases, payment is due within 60 days of the invoice date, and FabFrames Ltd is allowing Delta Q Bikes Ltd a PPD (Prompt Payment Discount) of 5% if the invoice is paid within 7 days of the invoice date. 30-day payment periods are more common, but 60 days is used here for the scenario.

The day book totals at the end of the time period are then transferred to the General Ledger:

Total	This is transferred to the **Payables Ledger Control Account.** This sum records the **liability** that is owed to suppliers and is a credit.
VAT	This is transferred to the **VAT Account.** This sum records the reduction of the **asset** that is owed from HMRC and is a debit, as it can be reclaimed from HMRC.
Net	This is transferred to the **Purchases Account.** This sum records the expected expenses from purchases and is a debit.

A key part of understanding the double-entry for the Purchases Day Book is that the sum of money in a transaction behaves in these three different ways simultaneously.

As well as being recorded in the General Ledger, the purchases will also be recorded in the supplier accounts in the Payables Ledger. The behaviour of the Payables Ledger and Payables Ledger Control Account are identical, as both accounts record the value of the liability (the purchase) still owed to the supplier.

General Ledger

The General Ledger, or Nominal Ledger, is where the main accounts of the business are located within the double-entry system.

A manual bookkeeping system will transfer totals from the day books to the double-entry bookkeeping system at regular intervals. In this case, the totals are transferred to the double-entry system at the end of the month.

In modern computerised bookkeeping systems, transfers to the General Ledger occur immediately when the details are entered into the accounting system rather than transferred at the end of the week or month, which is more common in manual systems.

The entry in the Payables Ledger Control Account will have a **credit** balance. As this is a liability account, the credit balance indicates that on January 31st, credit purchases of £2262.00 were entered into the account, and the same amount is owed to suppliers as a liability. PDB indicates that the information came from the Purchases Day Book.

Payables Ledger Control Account (2100)					
Debit £					Credit £
			31-01	**PDB**	**2,262.00**

The entry in the VAT Account (sometimes known as the VAT Control Account) indicates that £377.00 can be reclaimed on those purchases from HMRC.

VAT Account (2200)					
Debit £					Credit £
01-01	Bank	2,500.00			
01-01	Bank	2,250.00			
31-01	**PDB**	**377.00**			

The net amount is recorded in the Purchases Account. Businesses may have only one purchases account or use multiple accounts to record purchases of different types.

Purchases Account (5000)					
Debit £					Credit £
01-01	Bank	1,250.00			
30-01	**PDB**	**1,885.00**			

Payables Ledger

The Payables Ledger contains an account for each supplier from which the business buys on credit and maintains a list of individual transactions and how much is owed to a supplier at any given time. Entries in the Payables Ledger must be entered using the date of the original transactions rather than the end of the month. This is so that a correct record is made of when the liability is due to the supplier, to ensure that the agreed payment terms are met, and that payments are not made late.

Fab Frames Ltd (FAB001)					
Debit £					Credit £
			03-11	**PDB**	**1,080.00**

WonderWheels (WON001)					
Debit £					Credit £
			08-11	**PDB**	**900.00**

SuperSuspension (SUP001)					
Debit £					Credit £
			10-11	**PDB**	**282.00**

Purchases Returns

The following purchases returns have been recorded in the Purchases Returns Day Book for DeltaQ Bikes Ltd.

Purchases Returns Day Book						
Date	**Details**	**Credit note**	**PL Code**	**Net £**	**VAT £**	**Total £**
03-01	FabFrames Ltd	CRN215	FAB001	90.00	18.00	108.00
15-01	WonderWheels	PINC276	WON001	10.00	2.00	12.00
16-01	SuperSuspension	INVC561	SUP001	4.00	0.80	4.80
			TOTALS:	104.00	20.80	124.80

The day book totals are then transferred to the General Ledger as follows:

Total	This is transferred to the **Payables Ledger Control Account.** This sum records the **reduction of the liability** that is owed to suppliers and is a debit.
VAT	This is transferred to the **VAT Account.** This sum records the **reduction of the expense** that can be claimed from HMRC and is a credit, as it cannot be reclaimed.
Net	This is transferred to the **Purchases Returns Account.** This sum records the **reduction of the expense** from purchases and is a credit.

A key part of understanding the double-entry for the Purchases Returns Day Book is that the sum of money simultaneously behaves in these three different ways. Students often struggle with day books if they do not understand the triple nature of these transactions in terms of behaviour in the General Ledger.

As well as being recorded in the General Ledger, the purchases will also be recorded in the supplier accounts in the Payables Ledger. The behaviour of the Payables Ledger and Payables Ledger Control Account are identical, as both accounts record the value of the liability (the purchase) still owed to the supplier. The details PRDB are used to explain where the information came from.

The double-entry for a purchases return therefore will be as follows:

General Ledger

Payables Ledger Control Account (2100)					
Debit £					Credit £
31-01	**PRDB**	**124.80**	30-11	PDB	2,262.00

VAT Account (2200)					
Debit £					Credit £
01-01	Bank	2,500.00	**31-01**	**PRDB**	**20.80**
01-01	Bank	2,250.00			
31-01	PDB	377.00			

Purchases Returns Account (5050)					
Debit £					**Credit £**
			30-11	**PRDB**	**104.00**

A separate account is used for recording purchases and purchases returns, rather than recording the purchases returns on the credit side of the purchases account. This is better storytelling, as it enables anyone analysing the bookkeeping or the accounts to ascertain the level of purchases returns, which could be an indicator of a problem (e.g., poor quality of goods bought), whereas recording returns within the Purchases Account could make it harder to find such information.

Payables Ledger

Fab Frames Ltd (FAB001)					
Debit £					Credit £
03-01	**PRDB**	**108.00**	01-01	PDB	1,080.00

SuperSuspension (SUP001)					
Debit £					Credit £
14-01	**PRDB**	**4.80**	10-11	PDB	282.00

WonderWheels (WON001)					
Debit £					Credit £
15-01	**PRDB**	**12.00**	08-11	PDB	900.00

Discounts Received

The following discounts have been recorded in the Discounts Received Day book for DeltaQ Bikes Ltd.

Discounts Received Day Book						
Date	**Details**	**Credit note no:**	**PL Code**	**Net £**	**VAT £**	**Total £**
05-01	FabFrames Ltd	CRN218	FAB001	40.50	8.10	48.60
			TOTALS:	40.50	8.10	48.60

This discount received amount represents 5% of £972.00. The original invoice total from FabFrames Ltd was £1080.00. This was reduced by the credit note by £108.00 due to a damaged frame, making the final total due £972.00. The original invoice indicated a PPD (prompt payment discount) if it was paid within 7 days. The invoice was sent on January 1st and paid on January 5th, so a discount was appropriate.

The day book totals are then transferred to the General Ledger as follows:

Total	This is transferred to the **Payables Ledger Control Account.** This sum records the **reduction of the liability** that is owed to suppliers and is a debit.
VAT	This is transferred to the **VAT Account.** This sum records the **reduction of the expense** that can be claimed from HMRC and is a credit.
Net	This is transferred to the **Discounts Received Account.** This sum records the **amount of the reduction given by suppliers as an income** (expense reduction) and is a credit.

A key part of understanding the double-entry for the Discounts Received Day Book is that the sum of money simultaneously behaves in these different ways. Students often struggle with day books if they do not understand the triple nature of these transactions in terms of behaviour in the General Ledger.

As well as being recorded in the General Ledger, the discounts received will also be recorded in the supplier accounts in the Payables Ledger. The behaviour of the Payables Ledger and Payables Ledger Control Account are identical, as both accounts record the value of the liability (the purchase) still owed to the supplier.

The double-entry for a discount received therefore will be as follows:

General Ledger

The entries in the Payables Ledger Control Account cover both the amount of the discount *(£48.60)* and the actual amount paid by Delta Q Bikes Ltd to FabFrames Ltd *(£923.40).* This means that the liability from the invoice is now reduced to £0.00.

Payables Ledger Control Account (2100)					
Debit £					Credit £
31-01	PRDB	124.80	30-11	PDB	2,262.00
31-01	**DRDB**	**48.60**			
31-01	**Bank**	**923.40**			

VAT Account (2200)					
Debit £					Credit £
01-01	Bank	2,500.00	31-01	PRDB	20.80
01-01	Bank	2,250.00	**31-01**	**DRDB**	**8.10**
31-01	PDB	377.00			

Discounts Received Account (5009)					
Debit £					Credit £
			31-01	**DRDB**	**40.50**

Bank Account (1200)					
Debit *(dr)*		£	Credit *(cr)*		£
01-01	Capital	20,000.00	01-01	Machinery	15,000.00
01-01	Bank Loan	25,000.00	01-01	Raw Materials	13,500.00
			05-01	**PLCA**	**923.40**

Payables Ledger

Fab Frames Ltd (FAB001)					
Debit £					Credit £
03-01	PRDB	108.00	01-01	PDB	1,080.00
05-01	**DRDB**	**48.60**			
05-01	**Bank**	**923.40**			

Document Checking

Before a supplier is paid, it is vital to check that the correct amount is being paid and that there are no errors in the bookkeeping. Various documents form an important part of this process, particularly:

- Invoices
- Credit notes
- Statements of account
- Payables Ledger Control Account
- Payables Ledger (supplier account)

Invoices should be checked when they are received. They should be checked against the original purchase order to which they relate, and any issues or discrepancies raised with the supplier before proceeding further.

Any credit notes received should also be checked against the need for the credit note. A credit note may need to be checked against:

- Purchase order
- Invoice
- Goods received note (if goods were missing or damaged)

When a statement of account is received from the supplier, it should be checked against all of the relevant documents, and the double-entry bookkeeping records of the business in the Payables Ledger for that supplier, prior to any payment being authorised or made.

Common errors include:

- Invoices incorrectly calculated.
- Invoices with the wrong item or wrong quantity listed.
- Credit notes incorrectly calculated.
- Credit notes with the wrong item or wrong quantity listed.
- Statements of Account with extra or missing items.

These errors could potentially lead to the following discrepancies when making payments to suppliers:

- Underpayments or overpayments
- Incorrect discount taken
- Incorrect details given
- Timing differences (due to incorrect dates being recorded)
- Missing or duplicated transactions

The use of computerised accounting software helps to minimise the risk of errors occurring in the day books or double-entry bookkeeping, but the software is only as good as the bookkeeper who is entering the transactions, so due care is important when entering and checking information.

Delta Q Bikes Ltd have now received a Statement of Account from Fab Frames Ltd, which should be checked against the bookkeeping and bank records, as required.

Statement of account				
From: FabFrames Ltd 25 Meadowcroft Estate Ashwell AS19 2HF VAT No: GB145853235		**To:** Delta Q Bikes Ltd Unit 3b Ashwell Business Park Ashwell AS17 4BX VAT No: GB798204391		
Account: DEL001		**Date:** 31/01/2022		
Date	**Details**	**Debit £**	**Credit £**	**Balance £**
01/01/2022	Balance b/f			0.00
01/01/2022	Invoice FF431	1080.00		1080.00
03/01/2022	Credit note CRN215		108.00	972.00
Payments may be made electronically to FabFrames Ltd Sort code: 01-26-91 Account no: 45813290			**Total:**	£972.00

This statement of account will be checked against the following:

- The original purchase invoice
- The credit note
- The supplier account for Fab Frames Ltd in the Payables Ledger

Common features to look out for are:

- Invoice number
- Net prices (with or without bulk/trade discounts, which should be calculated correctly)
- VAT calculations & percentages
- Total calculation

Many of these cross-checks should be done when an invoice is first received, although it is also helpful to recheck an invoice against the statement of account once it is received.

The check between the invoice and the statement of account appears to show no errors, as the original value of the invoice and the invoice number are correctly recorded on the statement of account.

The amount on the credit note (£108.00) matches the amount on the statement of account. It is also the case that the credit note number (CRN215) is the same on both documents, so there are no errors here.

The final check is to look at the supplier account in the Payables Ledger.

The original supplier account is shown again here.

Fab Frames Ltd (FAB001)					
Debit £					Credit £
03-01	PRDB	108.00	01-01	PDB	1,080.00
05-01	**DRDB**	**48.60**			
05-01	**Bank**	**923.40**			

Fab Frames Ltd have made a mistake on the statement of account, as they have not listed the Prompt Payment Discount nor the payment of the balance, paid by Delta Q Bikes Ltd on the 5th of the month, and as shown in the supplier account in the bookkeeping of Delta Q Bikes Ltd.

Delta Q Bikes Ltd should contact Fab Frames Ltd and inform them of the mistake as soon as possible, confirming that Fab Frames Ltd have received the payment and acknowledge the Prompt Payment Discount, and that the account is now fully paid.

Another option is that Delta Q Bikes Ltd have recorded the discount received and the payment made but neglected to make the payment. A check should be made to confirm that the payment did take place.

A further, corrected, statement of account could be sent, or the adjustments would show on the statement of account next month.

This discrepancy might have been avoided if a remittance advice had been sent along with payment.

Remittance Advice

A document that has not been considered so far is a **Remittance Advice**. This document is often sent by a customer to a supplier to indicate what they have paid and to what items/invoices/credit notes it relates. A remittance advice may look like this, although styles may vary.

<table>
<tr><th colspan="4">Remittance Advice</th></tr>
<tr><td colspan="2">From:
Delta Q Bikes Ltd
Unit 3b
Ashwell Business Park
Ashwell
AS17 4BX</td><td colspan="2">To:
FabFrames Ltd
25 Meadowcroft Estate
Ashwell
AS19 2HF</td></tr>
<tr><td colspan="4">Date: 05/01/2022

A payment of £923.40 was made by bank transfer on 05/01/2022, relating to the following invoice and adjustments.</td></tr>
<tr><td>Date
01/01/22
03/01/22
05/01/22</td><td>Our Ref
PO452
PO452
PO452</td><td>Your Ref
FF431
CRN215
FF431 (PPD @ 5%)</td><td>Amount £
1080.00
(108.00)
(48.60)</td></tr>
</table>

Computerised accounting packages can produce a remittance advice as a document, which can then be printed to send to a supplier or via email.

A remittance advice is often sent:

1. As an attachment to an email to indicate that an electronic payment has been made, or
2. As a printed document sent along with a cheque to indicate the reason for the cheque.

More informally, a remittance advice may take the form of the accounts person at one company informing another accounts person at another company by email or phone that a payment has or is about to be made.

Analysed Purchases Day Book

A business that chooses to analyse its purchases at a deeper level within the bookkeeping may use an analysed day book. An analysed day book replaces the single net column (which would typically be the purchases account) with relevant columns for different purchase types.

For example, Morgan could choose to analyse purchases for standard bikes and e-bikes separately, in which case her analysed purchases day book could be set out in the following manner:

	Purchases Day Book						
Date	Details	Invoice	PL Code	Purchases - Bikes	Purchases – E-bikes	VAT £	Total £
			TOTALS:				

In an analysed day book, the VAT and Total columns would be recorded as usual, but the relevant purchases (net) would be used to signify the different categories of purchase, with each given a separate General Ledger code – for example, 5000, 5001.

It is common for businesses that make multiple product types to analyse purchases in this way, as it provides better storytelling regarding the cost of purchases for different parts of the business.

Account Balances

At the end of chapter 2, we had the following trial balance, indicating the balance of individual accounts in the General Ledger at that time:

Trial Balance Delta Q Bikes Ltd 1st January			
Nominal Code	Account	Debit £	Credit £
0010	Machinery	12,500.00	
1200	Bank	16,500.00	
2200	VAT	4,750.00	
2500	Bank Loan		25,000.00
3000	Capital		20,000.00
5000	Purchases	11,250.00	
	Total	**45,000.00**	**45,000.00**

Several transactions have now taken place, and a new trial balance is generated:

Trial Balance Delta Q Bikes Ltd January 31st			
Nominal Code	**Account**	**Debit £**	**Credit £**
0010	Machinery	12,500.00	
1200	**Bank**	**15,576.60**	
2100	**Payables Ledger Control Account**		**1,165.20**
2200	**VAT**	**5,098.10**	
2500	Bank Loan		25,000.00
3000	Capital		20,000.00
5000	**Purchases**	**13,135.00**	
5009	**Discounts Received**		**40.50**
5050	**Purchases Returns**		**104.00**
	Total	**46,309.70**	**46,309.70**

These changes are because of the following transactions that have taken place in this chapter, covering:

- Credit purchases
- Purchases returns
- Discounts received (including recording of eventual payment to the supplier)

Account	Debit £	Credit £
Payables Ledger Control Account		2,262.00
Purchases – Raw Materials	1,885.00	
VAT	377.00	
Payables Ledger Control Account	124.80	
Purchases Returns		104.00
VAT		20.80
Payables Ledger Control Account	48.60	
Discounts Received		40.50
VAT		8.10
Payables Ledger Control Account	923.40	
Bank		923.40

Note that the debit and credit sides of the trial balance still add up to the same amounts, meaning that it is likely to be free from errors. However, as you will see in the Principles of Bookkeeping Controls unit, there are valid reasons why a trial balance that balances is not necessarily correct.

It is also worth noting that the following supplier balances in the Payables Ledger also explain the balance of £1,165.20 in the Payables Ledger Control account:

Account	Debit £	Credit £
SuperSuspension		888.00
WonderWheels		277.20

No money is owed to FabFrames Ltd as the invoice (minus the credit note and minus the prompt payment discount) was paid in full.

Both the Payables Ledger Control Account (in summary format) and the Payables Ledger (with the details of individual transactions) tell the same story, of what is owed to suppliers at any given time as liabilities.

Digital Focus

Students should practice the following skills in computerised accounting software.

1. Adding a credit purchase to a supplier account.
2. Adding a purchase return to a supplier account.
3. Adding a discount received to a supplier account.
4. Recording a payment to a supplier.

This can most easily be done by entering the transactions listed in this chapter, setting up the various suppliers and then entering the transactions.

Accounting software will vary as to what compulsory details are required when setting up a supplier. Where possible, use details that you are given in the text here, but improvise with false addresses where necessary, which is acceptable as these are not actual companies. It is more about practising the processes involved.

You will need to add an invoice for adding a credit purchase, whereas for the purchase return and the discount received, these are done by adding credit notes.

The payment through the bank will require using the bank part of the software, and then selecting the relevant supplier. There are often options that distinguish between cash and credit transactions. A credit note will need to be created to account for the PPD.

Once the transactions have been entered, it will be worthwhile exploring the parts of the software that show:

- Account balances and lists of transactions for suppliers (the digital equivalent of the Payables Ledger).
- Payables Ledger Control Account (this may go by another name) for overall balances in the General Ledger.

Within most accounting software, you will not find something called the Payables Ledger (or the Receivables Ledger we will see in the next chapter), but there will be separate sections for customers and suppliers that will fulfil the same requirements.
In most accounting software, the Payables Ledger Control Account will be called either the Purchases Ledger Control Account, or the Creditors Control Account, although accounting software will often allow you to change the name to whatever you wish.

Summary

Making credit purchases involves the creation of a liability in the Payables Ledger Control Account, by making a credit entry in the account.

This also involves making a debit entry in the relevant Purchases Account and the VAT Account. The debit in the Purchases Account is because it is an expense, and the debit in the VAT Account is because the money can be reclaimed from HMRC.

A purchases return requires a debit entry in the Payables Ledger Control Account. This is because a purchases return involves the reduction of a liability, as less money will be paid to the supplier. The entry in the Purchases Return Account (opposite of a purchase) will be a credit, and the entry in the VAT Account will also be a credit, as it is a reduction of the amount of VAT that can be reclaimed from HMRC.

Discounts Received are a debit in the Payables Ledger Control Account as the discount received from a supplier reduces the amount of the liability owed to the supplier. It is a credit in the Discounts Received Account, as it behaves in a very similar way to income and reduces the expense of the purchase, and is a credit in the VAT Account as it reduces the amount that can be reclaimed from HMRC as less is being paid.

Fundamentally, a credit purchase is about the creation (purchase), reduction (purchase return, discount received) or elimination (payment to a supplier) of a liability.

Here, the term credit, as in credit purchase, means buy now pay later, as in 'buying on credit'. It has no immediate implications for the payment method eventually used, nor for whether the entry is a debit or credit in a particular account.

It should be noted that the double-entry for a credit purchase, purchase return, or discount received, is usually a two-stage process.

Stage 1
A double-entry transaction is recorded when the purchase is made, in order to record the liability owed to the supplier and any VAT implications.

Stage 2
A double-entry transaction is recorded when the payment is made. VAT is not recorded at this point as it is already recorded when the purchase is made. This is known as the accruals basis of accounting, which is studied further at level 3.

There may also be an intermediate stage requiring a double-entry transaction if a purchase return takes place, including any VAT implications, for example, for damaged or incorrect goods.

The credit purchase process can therefore be summarised in the following table.

In each case:

- The sum of the debits & credits will be equal.
- The VAT figure (if appropriate) will be the lowest of the three figures.
- The Control Account figure will be the highest of the figures when three figures/entries are involved.

Purchase		
	Debit	**Credit**
Purchases	✓	
VAT	✓	
Payables Ledger Control Account		✓
Purchase Return		
	Debit	**Credit**
Payables Ledger Control Account	✓	
Purchases Returns		✓
VAT		✓
Discount Received		
	Debit	**Credit**
Payables Ledger Control Account	✓	
Discounts Received		✓
VAT		✓
Payment of Invoice		
	Debit	Credit
Payables Ledger Control Account	✓	
Bank		✓

Skills & Knowledge Test – Chapter 3

QUESTION 18

For each of the following net amounts, calculate the amount of VAT at 20% and the Gross (total). All answers should be to the nearest pence and rounded down if appropriate.

Net £	VAT £	Total £
94.80		
124.32		
160.00		
245.95		
342.20		
1235.60		

QUESTION 19

For the following amounts that include VAT at 20%, calculate the net and the VAT. All amounts should be rounded down to the nearest pence.

Total £	Net £	VAT £
126.00		
78.60		
96.30		
108.00		
246.60		
585.00		

QUESTION 20

Record the following invoices in the Purchases Day book and then transfer the totals into the General Ledger and Payables Ledger. Account coding and balancing are not necessary.

Company	Date	Invoice no.	Price
Company A	01-02	Inv124	£100 exc. VAT
Company B	04-02	COBA12	£92 exc. VAT
Company C	05-02	GGA445	£476.20 exc. VAT

Purchases Day Book					
Date	**Details**	**Invoice no.**	**Net £**	**VAT £**	**Total £**
		TOTALS:			

General Ledger

Account:	
Debit £	Credit £

Account:	
Debit £	Credit £

Account:	
Debit £	Credit £

Payables Ledger

Account:	
Debit £	Credit £

Account:	
Debit £	Credit £

Account:	
Debit £	Credit £

QUESTION 21

Record the following invoices in the Purchases Returns Day book and then transfer the totals into the General Ledger and Payables Ledger. Account coding and balancing are not necessary.

Company	Date	Invoice no.	Price
Company A	08-02	CN234	£8.60 exc. VAT
Company B	11-02	CN118	£43.60 exc. VAT
Company C	13-02	CC42	£274.20 exc. VAT

Purchases Returns Day Book					
Date	Details	CN no.	Net £	VAT £	Total £
		TOTALS:			

General Ledger

Account:	
Debit £	Credit £

Account:	
Debit £	Credit £

Account:	
Debit £	Credit £

Payables Ledger

Account:	
Debit £	Credit £

Account:	
Debit £	Credit £

Account:	
Debit £	Credit £

QUESTION 22

Record the following invoices in the Discounts Received Day book and then transfer the totals into the General Ledger and Purchases Ledger. Account coding and balancing are not necessary.

Company	**Date**	**Invoice no.**	**Price**
Company A	11-02	CN18	£4.60 exc. VAT
Company B	19-02	CN431	£11.10 exc. VAT

Discounts Received Day Book					
Date	**Details**	**CN no.**	**Net £**	**VAT £**	**Total £**
		TOTALS:			

General Ledger

Account:	
Debit £	Credit £

Account:	
Debit £	Credit £

Account:	
Debit £	Credit £

Payables Ledger

Account:	
Debit £	Credit £

Account:	
Debit £	Credit £

QUESTION 23

For the following invoice and PPD % amounts, calculate the amount of (gross) discount that can be taken, and the (gross) amount to be paid.

Invoice amount £	**% PPD**	**Discount to be taken £**	**Amount to be paid £**
200.00	5		
150.00	2.5		
450.00	4		
620.00	10		
180.00	6		

QUESTION 24

The PPD discount amount (in £) should be deducted when calculating the initial value of an invoice.

True	
False	

QUESTION 25

A prompt payment discount of 5% on an invoice of 180.00 (inc. VAT) has been taken from a purchase from Company D.

What should be recorded in the General Ledger to record the discount?

Account	Amount	Debit	Credit

What should be recorded in the Payables Ledger to record the discount only?

Account	Amount	Debit	Credit

What should be recorded in the General Ledger to record the payment actually made from the bank?

Account	Amount	Debit	Credit

QUESTION 26

Match the statement to the ledger or account.

	Payables Ledger Control Account	Payables Ledger
Contains a summary of the transactions & balances of the supplier accounts.		
Contains details of individual transactions and balances for individual suppliers.		

QUESTION 27

Identify the discount type from the description.

	Trade	Bulk	PPD
A discount offered if payment on the invoice is made within a certain time period.			
A discount % offered to a particular customer on all orders.			
A discount offered for ordering more than a certain quantity or value of an item or items.			

QUESTION 28

The following codes have been assigned to suppliers, assign correct codes to the new suppliers.

Harton PLC	HAR001
Booknorth Ltd	BOK001
Bood Supplies	BOO002
Dixon Supplies	DIX001

New supplier	Account Code
Ashburton Paper Supplies	
Harmfield Plastics	

This section has been created for you should you wish to use it to make notes or for calculations.

Credit Sales

Introduction

Businesses use documents to facilitate the process of sales and purchases. These documents provide an important paper trail that can help resolve problems between the buyer (customer) and the seller (supplier) of goods and services.

Many of these documents are nowadays created and sent electronically (either by email or downloadable from a website) rather than on paper. Some documents are also in less common use than in the past. Bookkeepers need to be aware of and able to create and interpret these documents and understand their role in the buying & selling process.

The key sales & purchases documents are:

Document Types	
Price Quotation	A document provided by the seller of goods and services, outlining the price the buyer will pay should they place an order.
Purchase Order	A document provided by the buyer of goods and services, outlining to the seller the goods and services that they wish to buy.
Invoice	The key document provided by the seller, outlining the items sold, the cost of those items, and when/how the buyer should pay.
Goods Received Note	A document completed by the buyer, which acknowledges receipt of the goods purchased.
Credit Note	A document provided by the seller to the buyer when goods or services are returned or are incomplete and reduces the value of the invoice to which it relates.
Statement of Account	A document sent by the seller to the buyer outlining the balance of the account, and any related transactions.

These documents, and the remittance advice, have been considered in detail in the previous chapter. Some of these documents, notably the invoice and the credit note, will be considered again, this time from the perspective of selling to customers.

The exact layout of these documents will vary from business to business. The style of the documents in this book is one of many potential options. Many of these documents (for example, purchase orders, invoices & credit notes) can be generated automatically by computerised accounting software with customisable templates.

Before looking at the documents and processes around credit sales, let us remind ourselves of the scenario for this unit.

Scenario
Morgan has started a business making and selling bicycles. This business is called Delta Q Bikes Ltd and makes both standard and electric bicycles. Bicycles are sold to shops, who then sell them on to customers, and are also sold direct to customers by Delta Q Bikes Ltd via their online shop and website. Morgan has put some of her own money into the business (this is known as capital) as well as money from a friend and a bank loan (which are known as liabilities). She has rented a property from which to manufacture bikes and store them in a warehouse and has hired two other employees. Morgan has also invested in specialist machinery (an asset) for manufacturing the bikes. The business will use a double-entry bookkeeping system, which uses a series of day books (for credit sales and purchases) linked to a Receivables Ledger, a Payables Ledger, and the General Ledger. The business will buy components and other items from suppliers, which are known as credit purchases, and will sell finished goods to shops, which are known as credit sales. Cash sales to retail customers, from the online website, are also recorded. A cash book and petty cash book are used, both of which are books of prime entry and double-entry, and will record the money element of all purchases, expenses and income, as well as any drawings made by the owner.

This chapter will consider credit sales, looking at sales documents from the perspective of Delta Q Bikes Ltd as the business sells to customers on credit. Students can refresh their knowledge of the documents involved in the previous chapter on pages 49-54.

Students should be aware that if they are practising entering transactions into accounting software, the software will do the entries into the Receivables Ledger Control Account (which may go by another name) automatically, so students should not usually attempt to enter them in that account.

Recording Credit Sales

Businesses that sell on credit need a system of recording the value of sales. They need to be able to separately record:

- The value of the net sale.
- The amount of the VAT to be paid to or claimed from HMRC.
- The total amount of the asset owned (for a sale). This needs to be done both in the General Ledger and the Receivables Ledger.

Typically, this has been done with a series of day books as follows:

Sales Day Book (for credit sales)
Sales Returns Day Book (for credit sales returns)
Discounts Allowed Day Book (to record prompt payment discounts given)

Sales transactions are initially recorded in the relevant day book and then transferred to the correct accounts in the General Ledger.

The day books described above and the process of transferring to the ledger accounts described in the following pages are only for credit sales. Credit purchases, although a very similar process, were discussed in the previous chapter.

Credit sales = buy now, pay later. An invoice is sent with the goods, and the buyer pays within the prescribed payment period.

Cash sales = buy now, pay now. The payment takes place at the same time as transfer of ownership of the goods.

The term credit or cash refers to the nature of the transaction (buy now pay later or buy now pay now), not the payment method. The terms cash and credit can have multiple meanings in accountancy and bookkeeping. When transferring transactions from sales-related day books to ledgers, it is always the case that:

- There will be two credits and one debit, or two debits and one credit.
- The sum of the credits will equal the sum of the debits.
- One account will always be the Receivables Ledger Control Account.
- One account will always be the VAT Account.
- The other account will be named after the relevant day book.

Sales

The following sales have been recorded in the Sales Day Book for Delta Q Bikes Ltd.

Sales Day Book						
Date	**Details**	**Invoice**	**RL Code**	**Net £**	**VAT £**	**Total £**
02-02	Northlynch Bikes	DQB001	NOR001	1500.00	300.00	1800.00
04-02	Westernpool Cycles	DQB002	WES001	625.00	125.00	750.00
			TOTALS:	2125.00	425.00	2550.00

A column is included here to show the Receivables Ledger account code for each supplier. A separate row or section could also include the General Ledger codes for the Net, VAT & Total columns if desired. A separate row or section could also include the General Ledger codes for the Net, VAT & Total columns if desired. There could also be separate net columns if there were more than one sales category. This would then be referred to as an analysed day book.

For each of these sales, payment is due within 30 days of the date of the invoice, and Delta Q Bikes Ltd are allowing both businesses a PPD (Prompt Payment Discount) of 2.5% if the invoice is paid within 7 days of the invoice total.

Businesses will usually have a policy for offering discounts, which may be laid out in their financial policy documents, outlining the conditions under which customers may, or may not, be offered discounts. This may include PPD, trade and bulk discounts. This means that sales personnel can offer the correct discounts when available.

The day book totals at the end of the week or month are then transferred to the General Ledger as follows:

Total	This is transferred to the **Receivables Ledger Control Account.** This sum records the **asset** that is owed by customers and is a debit.
VAT	This is transferred to the **VAT Account.** This sum records the **liability** that is owed to HMRC and is a credit.
Net	This is transferred to the **Sales Account*.** This sum records the expected **income** from sales and is a credit.

**in this case, the Sales – Shops account.*

A key part of understanding the double-entry for the Sales Day Book is that the sum of money behaves in these three different ways simultaneously.

As well as being recorded in the General Ledger, the sales will also be recorded in the customer accounts in the Receivables Ledger. The behaviour of the Receivables Ledger and Receivables Ledger Control Account are identical, as both accounts record the value of the asset (the sale) still owed by the customer.

General Ledger

The General Ledger, or Nominal Ledger, is where the main accounts of the business are located within the double-entry system.

In a manual bookkeeping system, totals from the day books will be transferred to the double-entry bookkeeping system at regular intervals. In this case, the totals are transferred to the double-entry system at the end of the month.

In modern computerised bookkeeping systems, transfers to the General Ledger occur when the details are first entered into the accounting system rather than transferred at the end of the month.

The entry in the Receivables Ledger Control Account will have a **debit** balance. As this is an asset account, the debit balance indicates that on January 31st, credit sales of £2550.00 were entered into the account, and the same amount is owed by customers as an asset. SDB indicates that the information came from the Sales Day Book.

Receivables Ledger Control Account (2110)					
Debit £					Credit £
31-01	**SDB**	**2550.00**			

The entry in the VAT Account (sometimes known as the VAT Control Account) indicates that £425.00 must be paid on these sales to HMRC.

When looking at the transfer of the total of the VAT column from the Sales Day Book to the VAT Account, note that the account was balanced at the end of the month.

The difference between the two sides was entered as the balance carried down on January 31st, the two columns were then added up to confirm that the totals were the same, then the difference between the two columns (the balance of the account) was entered on the opposite side, the debit side, on the February 1st, indicating an amount that can be reclaimed from HMRC.

VAT Account (2200)					
Debit £					Credit £
01-01	Bank	2,500.00	31-01	PRDB	20.80
01-01	Bank	2,250.00	31-01	DRDB	8.10
31-01	PDB	377.00	31-01	Balance c/d	5,098.10
		5,127.00			5,127.00
01-02	Balance b/d	5,098.10	**28-02**	**SDB**	**425.00**

The net amount is recorded in a sales account, in this case, the Sales – Shops Account. Businesses may have only one sales account, or they may use multiple accounts to record sales of different types.

Sales – Shops Account (4000)					
Debit £					Credit £
			28-02	**SDB**	**2,125.00**

Receivables Ledger

The Receivables Ledger contains an account for each customer to which the business sells on credit and maintains a list of individual transactions and how much is owed by a customer at any given time. Entries in the Receivables Ledger must be entered using the date of the original transactions rather than the end of the month. This is so that a correct record is made of when the asset is due from the customer, to ensure that the agreed payment terms are met, and payments are not received late.

Northlynch Bikes (NOR001)					
Debit £					Credit £
02-02	**SDB**	**1800.00**			

Westernpool Cycles (WES001)	
Debit £	Credit £
04-02 SDB 750.00	

Sales Returns

The following sales returns have been recorded in the Sales Returns Day Book for DeltaQ Bikes Ltd.

Sales Returns Day Book						
Date	**Details**	**Credit note**	**RL Code**	**Net £**	**VAT £**	**Total £**
07-02	Westernpool Cycles	CN001	WES001	110.00	22.00	132.00
			TOTALS:	110.00	22.00	132.00

The day book totals are then transferred to the General Ledger as follows:

Total	This is transferred to the **Receivables Ledger Control Account.** This sum records the **reduction of the asset** that is owed to suppliers and is a credit.
VAT	This is transferred to the **VAT Account.** This sum records the **reduction of the liability** that is owed to HMRC and is a debit.
Net	This is transferred to the **Sales Returns Account.** This sum records the **reduction of the income** from purchases and is a debit.

A key part of understanding the double-entry for the Sales Returns Day Book is that the sum of money behaves in these three different ways simultaneously. Students often struggle with day books if they do not understand the triple-nature of these transactions in terms of behaviour in the General Ledger.

As well as being recorded in the General Ledger, the sales will also be recorded in the customer accounts in the Receivables Ledger. The behaviour of the Receivables Ledger and

Receivables Ledger Control Account are identical, as both accounts record the value of the asset (the sale) still owed by the customer. The details SRDB are used to explain where the information came from.

The double-entry for a sales return therefore will be as follows:

General Ledger

Receivables Ledger Control Account (2110)					
Debit £					Credit £
31-01	SDB	2550.00	**28-02**	**SRDB**	**132.00**

VAT Account (2200)					
Debit £					Credit £
01-01	Bank	2,500.00	31-01	PRDB	20.80
01-01	Bank	2,250.00	31-01	DRDB	8.10
31-01	PDB	377.00	31-01	Balance c/d	5,098.10
		5,127.00			5,127.00
01-02	Balance b/d	5,098.10	28-02	SDB	425.00
28-02	**SRDB**	**22.00**			

Sales Returns Account (4050)					
Debit £					Credit £
			30-11	**SRDB**	**110.00**

Receivables Ledger

Westernpool Cycles (WES001)			
Debit £			Credit £
04-02 SDB	750.00	**07-02 SRDB**	**132.00**

Discounts Allowed

The following discounts have been recorded in the Discounts Allowed Day book for Delta Q Bikes Ltd.

Discounts Allowed Day Book						
Date	**Details**	**Credit note no:**	**SL Code**	**Net £**	**VAT £**	**Total £**
08-02	Northlynch Bikes	CN002	NOR001	37.50	7.50	45.00
			TOTALS:	37.50	7.50	45.00

This discount allowed amount represents 2.5% of £1800.00, the amount of the original invoice, or £45.00.

The invoice was sent on the 4th of February and paid on February 8th so therefore a discount was appropriate.

The day book totals are then transferred to the General Ledger as follows:

Total	This is transferred to the **Receivables Ledger Control Account.** This sum records the *reduction of the **asset*** that is owed by customers and is a credit.
VAT	This is transferred to the **VAT Account.** This sum records the *reduction of the **liability*** that is owed to HMRC and is a debit.
Net	This is transferred to the **Discounts Allowed Account.** This sum records the **amount of the reduction given to customers as an expense** (income reduction) and is a debit.

A key part of understanding the double-entry for the Discounts Allowed Day Book is that the sum of money behaves in these different ways simultaneously. Students often struggle with day books if they do not understand the triple-nature of these transactions in terms of behaviour in the General Ledger.

As well as being recorded in the General Ledger, the discounts allowed will also be recorded in the customer accounts in the Receivables Ledger. The behaviour of the Receivables Ledger and Receivables Ledger Control Account are identical, as both accounts record the value of the asset *(the sale)* still owed by the customer.

The double-entry for a discount allowed therefore will be as follows:

General Ledger

The entries in the Receivables Ledger Control Account cover both the amount of the discount *(£45.00)* and the actual amount paid by Northlynch Bikes to Delta Q Bikes Ltd (£1755.00). This means that the asset from the invoice is now reduced to £0.00.

Receivables Ledger Control Account (2110)					
Debit £					Credit £
31-01	SDB	2550.00	**08-02**	**Bank**	**1755.00**
			28-02	SRDB	132.00
			28-02	**DADB**	**45.00**

VAT Account (2200)					
Debit £					Credit £
01-01	Bank	2,500.00	31-01	PRDB	20.80
01-01	Bank	2,250.00	31-01	DRDB	8.10
31-01	PDB	377.00	31-01	Balance c/d	5,098.10
		5,127.00			5,127.00
01-02	Balance b/d	5,098.10	28-02	SDB	425.00
28-02	SRDB	22.00			
28-02	**DADB**	**7.50**			

Discounts Allowed Account (4009)			
Debit £			Credit £
28-02	**DADB**	**37.50**	

Bank Account (1200)					
Debit *(dr)*		£	Credit *(cr)*		£
01-01	Capital	20,000.00	01-01	Machinery	15,000.00
01-01	Bank Loan	25,000.00	01-01	Raw Materials	13,500.00
			05-01	PLCA	923.40
			31-01	Balance c/d	15,576.60
		45,000.00			45,000.00
01-02	Balance b/d	15,576.60			
08-02	**RLCA**	**1,755.00**			

As with the VAT Account earlier in the chapter, the Bank Account has been balanced at the end of January.

Receivables Ledger

Northlynch Bikes (NOR001)					
Debit £					Credit £
02-02	SDB	1,800.00	**08-02**	**DADB**	**45.00**
			08-02	**Bank**	**1,755.00**

If the Northlynch Bikes account in the Receivables Ledger were now balanced, it would show a balance of £0.00 (the difference between the two sides) as the invoice has been paid, minus the allowance for the prompt payment discount given to the customer.

The account of Westernpool Cycles has not yet been settled.

Document Checking

When a customer pays, it is vital to check that the correct amount is being paid and that there are no errors in the bookkeeping. Various documents form an important part of this process, particularly:

- Invoices
- Credit notes
- Statements of account

Payments should be checked when they are received. They should be checked against the original invoice to which they relate, as well as any related credit notes, and any issues or discrepancies raised with the customer. They should also be checked against the customer account in the Receivables Ledger.

Common errors include:

- Underpayments
- Overpayments
- Items missing from payments
- Disputed items

The use of computerised accounting software helps to minimise the risk of errors occurring in the day books or double-entry bookkeeping, but the software is only as good as the bookkeeper who is entering the transactions, so due care is important when entering and checking information.

If a remittance advice has been received from a customer, either before or at the same time as payment has been received, it should be checked against what is expected from the customer.

Modern accounting software often allows for payments received to not only be entered into the accounting software, but also assigned against particular transactions, such as:

- Opening balances
- Invoices
- Credit notes

If a prompt payment discount has been correctly taken by a customer, then a credit note may need to be created and sent to the customer to ensure that the paperwork and the bookkeeping are complete.

It is sometimes the case that customers will pay off part of what is owed, for example, paying off part of an opening balance or only part of any invoice, paying off the rest at a later date. In computerised accounting systems, part payments can easily be assigned to particular balances, invoices or credit notes to show not just how much money is still owed, but against which transactions amounts are still owed.

Analysed Sales Day Book

A business that chooses to analyse its sales at a deeper level within the bookkeeping may use an analysed day book. An analysed day book replaces the single net column (which would normally be the sales account) with relevant columns for different purchase types.

For example, Morgan could choose to analyse sales for normal bikes and e-bikes separately, in which case her analysed sales day book could be set out in the following manner:

	Sales Day Book						
Date	**Details**	**Invoice**	**PL Code**	**Sales - Bikes**	**Sales - E-bikes**	**VAT £**	**Total £**
			TOTALS:				

In an analysed day book, the VAT and Total columns would be recorded as normal, but the relevant purchases (net) would be used to signify the different categories of sale, with each given a separate General Ledger code – for example, 4000, 4001.

It is common for businesses that sell multiple product types to analyse in this way, as it provides better storytelling regarding the sales income for different parts of the business.

Account Balances

At the end of chapter 3, we had the following trial balance, indicating the balance of individual accounts in the General Ledger at that time:

Trial Balance **Delta Q Bikes Ltd** **January 31st**			
Nominal Code	Account	Debit £	Credit £
0010	Machinery	12,500.00	
1200	Bank	15,576.60	
2100	Payables Ledger Control Account		1,165.20
2200	VAT	5,098.10	
2500	Bank Loan		25,000.00
3000	Capital		20,000.00
5000	Purchases	13,135.00	
5009	Discounts Received		40.50
5050	Purchases Returns		104.00
	Total	46,309.70	46,309.70

By now, students should be starting to understand that the trial balance is made up of a list of all of the accounts in the General Ledger for which the balance is not £0.00, clearly listing the balance for each account, as well as whether it is a debit or a credit balance.

In this trial balance, each account code in the General Ledger is also listed. In this case, the trial balance is listed in the order of the nominal code *(from 0001 to 9999),* but a trial balance can also be listed alphabetically if necessary.

A number of transactions have taken place in this chapter, which means that the new trial balance at the end of February is as follows:

Trial Balance Delta Q Bikes Ltd February 28th			
Nominal Code	Account	Debit £	Credit £
0010	Machinery –	12,500.00	
1200	**Bank**	**17,331.60**	
2100	Payables Ledger Control Account		1,165.20
2110	**Receivables Ledger Control Account**	**618.00**	
2200	**VAT**	**4,702.60**	
2500	Bank Loan		25,000.00
3000	Capital		20,000.00
4000	**Sales - Shops**		**2,125.00**
4009	**Discounts Allowed**	**37.50**	
4050	**Sales Returns**	**110.00**	
5000	Purchases	13,135.00	
5009	Discounts Received		40.50
5050	Purchases Returns		104.00
	Total	**48,434.70**	**48,434.70**

These changes are because of the following transactions that have taken place in this chapter, covering:

- Credit sales
- Sales returns
- Discounts allowed (including recording of eventual receipt from customer)

Account	Debit £	Credit £
Receivables Ledger Control Account	2,550.00	
Sales - Shops		2,125.00
VAT		425.00
Receivables Ledger Control Account		132.00
Sales Returns	110.00	
VAT	22.00	
Receivables Ledger Control Account		45.00
Discounts Allowed	37.50	
VAT	7.50	
Receivables Ledger Control Account		923.40
Bank	923.40	

Note that the debit and credit sides of the trial balance still add up, meaning that it is likely to be free from errors. However, as you will see in the Principles of Bookkeeping Controls unit, there are valid reasons why a trial balance that balances is not necessarily correct.

It is also worth noting that the balance of £618.00 in the Receivables Ledger Control account is also explained by the following customer balance in the Receivables Ledger:

Account	Debit £	Credit £
Westernpool Cycles	618.00	

No money is owed by Northlynch Bikes as the invoice (minus the prompt payment discount) was paid in full.

Both the Receivables Ledger Control Account (in summary format) and the Receivables Ledger (with the details of individual transactions) tell the same story, of what is owed by customers at any given time as assets.

Digital Focus

Students should practice the following skills in computerised accounting software.

1. Adding a credit sale to a customer account.
2. Adding a sales return to a customer account.
3. Adding a discount allowed to a customer account.
4. Recording a payment received from a customer.

This can most easily be done by entering the transactions that are listed in this chapter, setting up the various customers and then entering the transactions.

Accounting software will vary as to what compulsory details are required when setting up a customer. Where possible, use details that you are given in the text here, but improvise with false addresses where necessary, which is acceptable as these are not real companies.

For adding a credit sale, you will need to add an invoice, whereas for the sales return and the discount allowed, these are done by adding credit notes.

The receipt through the bank will require using the bank part of the software, and then selecting the relevant customer. A credit note will need to be created to account for the PPD.

Once the transactions have been entered, it will be worthwhile exploring the parts of the software that show:

- Account balances and lists of transactions for customers (the digital equivalent of the Receivables Ledger).
- Receivables Ledger Control Account (this may go by another name) for overall balances in the General Ledger.

Within most accounting software, you will not find something called the Receivables Ledger (or the Payables Ledger), but there will be separate sections for customers and suppliers that will fulfil the same requirements.
In most accounting software, the Receivables Ledger Control Account will be called either the Sales Ledger Control Account, or the Debtors Control Account, although accounting software will often allow you to change the name to whatever you wish.

Summary

Making credit sales involves the creation of an asset in the Receivables Ledger Control Account, by making a debit entry in the account.

This also involves making a credit entry in the relevant Sales Account and the VAT Account. The credit in the Sales Account is because it is an income, and the credit in the VAT Account is a liability to be paid to HMRC.

A sales return requires a credit entry in the Receivables Ledger Control Account. This is because a sales return involves the reduction of an asset, as less money will be owed by the customer. The entry in the Sales Returns Account (opposite of a sale) will be a debit, and the entry in the VAT Account will also be a debit, as it is a reduction of the amount of VAT to be paid to HMRC.

Discounts allowed are a credit in the Receivables Ledger Control Account as the discount allowed to a customer reduces the amount of the asset owed by the customer. It is a debit in the Discounts Allowed Account, as it behaves in a very similar way to an expense and reduces the income of the sale, and is a debit in the VAT Account as it reduces the amount of the liability owed to HMRC.

Fundamentally, a credit sale is about the creation (sale), reduction (sales return, discount allowed) or elimination (receipt from a customer) of an asset.

Here, the term credit, as in credit sale, means buy now pay later, as in 'buying on credit'. It has no immediate implications for the payment method eventually used, nor for whether the entry is a debit or credit in a particular account.

It should be noted that the double-entry for a credit sale, sales return, or discount allowed, is a two-stage process.

Stage 1
A double-entry transaction is recorded when the sale is made to record the asset owed by the customer and any VAT implications.

Stage 2
A double-entry transaction is recorded when the receipt is received. VAT is not recorded at this point as it is already recorded when the sale is made. This is known as the accruals basis of accounting, which is studied further at level 3.

There may also be an intermediate stage requiring a double-entry transaction if a sales return takes place, including any VAT implications, for example, for damaged or incorrect goods.

The credit sale process can therefore be summarised in the following table.

In each case:

- The sum of the debits & credits will be equal.
- The VAT figure (if appropriate) will be the lowest of the three figures.
- The Control Account figure will be the highest of the figures when three figures/entries are involved.

Sales		
	Debit	**Credit**
Sales		✓
VAT		✓
Receivables Ledger Control Account	✓	
Sales Return		
	Debit	**Credit**
Receivables Ledger Control Account		✓
Sales Returns	✓	
VAT	✓	
Discount Allowed		
	Debit	**Credit**
Receivables Ledger Control Account		✓
Discounts Allowed	✓	
VAT	✓	
Payment of Invoice Received		
	Debit	Credit
Receivables Ledger Control Account		✓
Bank	✓	

Skills & Knowledge Test – Chapter 4

QUESTION 29

Record the following invoices in the Sales Day book and then transfer the totals into the General Ledger and Receivables Ledger. Account coding and balancing are not necessary.

Company	Date	Invoice no.	Price
Company D	08-02	INV001	£120 exc. VAT
Company E	11-02	INV002	£84 exc. VAT
Company F	19-02	INV003	£91.20 exc. VAT

Sales Day Book					
Date	**Details**	**Invoice no.**	**Net £**	**VAT £**	**Total £**
		TOTALS:			

General Ledger

Account:	
Debit £	Credit £

Account:	
Debit £	Credit £

Account:	
Debit £	Credit £

Receivables Ledger

Account:	
Debit £	Credit £

Account:	
Debit £	Credit £

Account:	
Debit £	Credit £

QUESTION 30

Record the following invoices in the Sales Returns Day book and then transfer the totals into the General Ledger and Receivables Ledger. Account coding and balancing are not necessary.

Company	**Date**	**Invoice no.**	**Price**
Company D	14-02	CN001	£7.40 exc. VAT
Company E	17-02	CN002	£11 exc. VAT
Company F	18-02	CN003	£44.20 exc. VAT

Sales Returns Day Book					
Date	**Details**	**CN no.**	**Net £**	**VAT £**	**Total £**
		TOTALS:			

General Ledger

Account:	
Debit £	Credit £

Account:	
Debit £	Credit £

Account:	
Debit £	Credit £

Receivables Ledger

Account:	
Debit £	Credit £

Account:	
Debit £	Credit £

Account:	
Debit £	Credit £

QUESTION 31

Record the following invoices in the Discounts Allowed Day book and then transfer the totals into the General Ledger and Receivables Ledger. Account coding and balancing are not necessary.

Company	**Date**	**Invoice no.**	**Price**
Company D	24-02	CN004	£1.20 exc. VAT
Company E	26-02	CN005	£10.60 exc. VAT

Discounts Allowed Day Book					
Date	**Details**	**CN no.**	**Net £**	**VAT £**	**Total £**
		TOTALS:			

General Ledger

Account:	
Debit £	Credit £

Account:	
Debit £	Credit £

Account:	
Debit £	Credit £

Receivables Ledger

Account:	
Debit £	Credit £

Account:	
Debit £	Credit £

QUESTION 32

For the following invoice and PPD % amounts, calculate the amount of (gross) discount that can be taken, and the (gross) amount to be received.

Invoice amount £	% PPD	Discount to be taken £	Amount to be received £
180.00	4		
250.00	5		
100.00	2.5		
240.00	6		
175.00	2		

QUESTION 33

A prompt payment discount of 3% on an invoice of £280.00 (inc. VAT) has been taken from a sale to Company D.

What should be recorded in the General Ledger to record the discount?

Account	Amount	Debit	Credit

What should be recorded in the Receivables Ledger to record the payment actually received into the bank?

Account	Amount	Debit	Credit

What should be recorded in the General Ledger to record the payment actually received?

Account	Amount	Debit	Credit

QUESTION 34

Match the statement to the ledger or account.

	Receivables Ledger Control Account	Receivables Ledger
Contains a summary of the transactions & balances of the customer accounts.		
Contains details of individual transactions and balances for individual customers.		

This section has been created for you should you wish to use it to make notes or for calculations.

The Cash Book

Introduction

Delta Q Bikes Ltd uses a Bank Account, an account in the General Ledger, that mirrors the behaviour of the actual business bank account, to record money coming in and out of the bank.

Here is that Bank Account in the General Ledger, with the transactions examined in previous chapters:

Bank Account (1200)					
Debit *(dr)*		£	Credit *(cr)*		£
01-01	Capital	20,000.00	01-01	Machinery	15,000.00
01-01	Bank Loan	25,000.00	01-01	Raw Materials	13,500.00
			05-01	PLCA	923.40
			31-01	Balance c/d	15,576.60
		45,000.00			45,000.00
01-02	Balance b/d	15,576.60	**28-02**	**Balance c/d**	**17,331.60**
08-02	RLCA	1,755.00			
		17,331.60			**17,331.60**
01-03	**Balance b/d**	**17,331.60**			

The account has been balanced as the business has reached the end of February, its second month of trading. The account has been balanced at the end of January and February. You are not expected to balance more than one period of time at level 2, but seeing the process helps to show how it works in balancing the books of the business on a regular basis.

However, as we shall now see, a business may use other mechanisms for recording the money coming in and out of the bank, as well as recording cash. For this, businesses may use a Cash Book.

The Cash Book and the Petty Cash Book are the main books for entering money paid out of and received into the business. The Cash Book will record cash coming in and out of the business (except for petty cash), as well as recording money coming in and out of the bank.

The Petty Cash Book will record smaller amounts of cash coming in and out of the business and will be examined in chapter 6.

For the purposes of AAT level 2 studies, both the Cash Book and the Petty Cash Book will function as both a book of prime entry (similar to a day book) as well as double-entry bookkeeping.

Before looking at the Cash Book and seeing how the previous transactions in this case study are applied to it, let us remind ourselves of the scenario for this unit.

Scenario
Morgan has started a business making and selling bicycles. This business is called Delta Q Bikes Ltd and makes both standard and electric bicycles. Bicycles are sold to shops, who then sell them on to customers, and are also sold direct to customers by Delta Q Bikes Ltd via their online shop and website. Morgan has put some of her own money into the business (this is known as capital) as well as money from a friend and a bank loan (which are known as liabilities). She has rented a property from which to manufacture bikes and store them in a warehouse and has hired two other employees. Morgan has also invested in specialist machinery (an asset) for manufacturing the bikes. The business will use a double-entry bookkeeping system, which uses a series of day books (for credit sales and purchases) linked to a Receivables Ledger, a Payables Ledger, and the General Ledger. The business will buy components and other items from suppliers, which are known as credit purchases, and will sell finished goods to shops, which are known as credit sales. Cash sales to retail customers, from the online website, are also recorded. A Cash Book and Petty Cash Book are used, both of which are books of prime entry and double-entry, and will record the money element of all purchases, expenses and income, as well as any drawings made by the owner.

Cash Book

The Cash Book is the book of prime entry and the double-entry bookkeeping for most transactions involving income and expenditure in the business. The exception, which will be examined in chapter 6, is the Petty Cash Book.

In many modern computerised accounting systems, there may not be a Cash Book, but rather there will be a Cash Account and a Bank Account in the General Ledger. However, some accounting software still allows specifically for a Cash Book.

In a larger business or financial department, there may be a Cashier who has the prime responsibility for the Cash Book.

In a manual accounting system, the Cash Book is typically laid out in the following manner:

Cash Book							
Date	**Details**	**Cash**	**Bank**	**Date**	**Details**	**Cash**	**Bank**

This is a very basic layout to help to initially understand how the Cash Book works and will be added to during the case study.

As with other double-entry accounts, there is a debit and a credit side, with space for multiple transactions on each side.

What is different with the Cash Book is that rather than just one place for entering the amount on each side, there are separate columns for cash and bank.

This is because you may have cash coming in and out of the business, as well as having both bank payments and receipts, so extra columns are required to keep track of cash and bank payments/receipts separately.

Because of these extra columns, the Cash Book will need to be balanced twice, once for the cash columns, and once for the bank columns. The Cash and Bank columns fulfil the role of double-entry, and no further double-entry is required for those columns in this case.

Here is how the Cash Book may have looked for Delta Q Bikes Ltd after the first month of trading, if they had used a Cash Book instead of a Bank Account in the General Ledger.

Date	Details	Cash	Bank	Date	Details	Cash	Bank
01-01	Capital		10,000.00	01-01	Machinery		15,000.00
01-01	Bank Loan		25,000.00	01-01	Purchases		13,500.00
				05-01	PLCA		923.40
				31-01	Balance c/d		15,576.60
			45,000.00				45,000.00
01-02	Balance b/d		15,576.60				

There are no entries in the Cash columns, as there have not yet been any transactions involving cash.

The behaviour of the Cash Book is the same as that of the Bank Account, as seen in earlier chapters, in that it follows Rule 1.

Money In =	**Money Out =**
Debit	Credit

Analysed Cash Book

It is common to use an analysed Cash Book, which means that as well as columns for Cash and Bank, which are double-entry, a business can be free to use other columns as suits the business best. These analysed columns are prime entry rather than double-entry and require a further entry in the General Ledger in the relevant account.

For AAT assessments, you will often be presented with either the debit or the credit side of the Cash Book, but rarely both side by side. This convention will also be followed here.

Analysed columns for the debit and credit sides have been added for:

- Trade receivables/Trade payables
- VAT
- Online sales (these are for online sales via the website)/cash purchases)
- Other income/expenses

For further ease of use in this study, we will break each Cash Book into one 'page' per month, as this is the style that is seen in assessments.

Firstly, the debit side of the Cash Book for January:

Cash Book – Debit £							
Date	**Details**	**Cash**	**Bank**	**Trade Receivables**	**VAT**	**Cash Sales**	**Other Income**
01-01	Capital		10,000.00				
01-01	Bank Loan		25,000.00				
			45,000.00				
01-02	Balance b/d		15,576.60				
			TOTALS:				

There are no numbers in the analysed columns, so there are no numbers to transfer to the double-entry bookkeeping. The balance c/d part of the balancing would be shown on the credit side, as will be seen momentarily.

Secondly, the credit side of the Cash Book for January:

Cash Book – Credit £							
Date	**Details**	**Cash**	**Bank**	**Trade Payables**	**VAT**	**Cash purchases**	**Other Expenses**
01-01	Machinery		15,000.00		2,500.00	12,500.00	
01-01	Purchases		13,500.00		2,250.00	11,250.00	
05-01	FabFrames Ltd		923.40	923.40			
31-01	Balance c/d		15,576.60				
			45,000.00				
			TOTALS:	923.40	4,750.00	28,500.00	

In this scenario, the £923.40 in the Trade Payables column would be transferred to the relevant account (Payables Ledger Control Account) at the end of the month.

The figures for machinery and purchases would also be transferred, if necessary, as well as their VAT equivalents. However, we saw in an earlier chapter that this was already done as part of the opening entries of the business.

No VAT is recorded for the payment made to FabFrames Ltd, as the VAT was recorded at the time the purchase was made, and only needs recording once.

A similar process can be seen for the month of February. There are no entries in the Cash columns on either the debit or the credit side as there have not yet been any cash (notes and coins) transactions to record.

Firstly, the debit side of the Cash Book for February:

Cash Book – Debit £							
Date	**Details**	**Cash**	**Bank**	**Trade Receivables**	**VAT**	**Cash Sales**	**Other Income**
01-02	Balance b/d		15.576.60				
08-02	Northlynch Bikes		1,755.00	1,755.00			
			17,331.60				
01-03	Balance b/d		17,331.60				
			TOTALS:	1,755.00			

The total of the Trade Receivables column would be transferred to the Receivables Ledger Control Account at the end of the month. There are no other entries to be made.

Secondly, the credit side of the Cash Book for February:

Cash Book – Credit £							
Date	**Details**	**Cash**	**Bank**	**Trade Payables**	**VAT**	**Cash purchases**	**Other Expenses**
01-02	Balance c/d		17,331.60				
			17,331.60				
			TOTALS:				

There have been no payments out of the bank during February, so there are no entries in the analysed columns, and there is just the balance carried down.

Sometimes, the Cash Book may include columns for discounts allowed (debit side) or discounts received (credit side) so the discount can be recorded in the Cash Book. However, as a discount is not a real sum of money (rather, it is a discount from the real sum), it is not required.

The Cash Book in this chapter will be studied further by considering a range of transactions that Delta Q Bikes Ltd will undertake in the month of March. These will be:

Payments

- Payments made to credit suppliers
- Wages
- Insurance
- Rent
- Bank charges
- Drawings

Morgan will also withdraw £500 from the bank to keep within the business, some of which will be used for petty cash.

Receipts

- Payments received from credit customers
- Online sales
- Bank interest received

Cash Book Payments

For recording cash & bank payments in the Cash Book, and for transferring those payments to the General Ledger, there are two important points to note:

1. The entries in the Cash and Bank columns are complete, and form one half of the double-entry transaction.
2. The entries in the analysed columns are not double-entry and will form the second half of the double-entry transaction once transferred into the General Ledger.

This is because the Cash Book is both a book of prime entry (analysed columns) and double-entry (Cash & Bank columns).

For analysed columns on the credit side of the Cash Book, the relevant double-entry must take place on the debit side of the account. This is because the credit part of the transaction is recorded in the cash or bank column.

For Delta Q Bikes Ltd, the following credit payments to suppliers are outstanding:

Account	Debit £	Credit £
SuperSuspension		888.00
WonderWheels		277.20

These are both paid on March 5th, with the following entries in the Cash Book:

Cash Book – Credit £							
Date	**Details**	**Cash**	**Bank**	**Trade Payables**	**VAT**	**Cash purchases**	**Other Expenses**
05-03	**Super Suspension**		**888.00**	**888.00**			
05-03	**WonderWheels**		**277.20**	**277.20**			
			TOTALS:				

No VAT is recorded, as this was already recorded at the time of purchase. These will require the following entries in the General Ledger and Payables Ledger:

General Ledger

Payables Ledger Control Account (2100)					
Debit £					Credit £
31-01	PRDB	124.80	30-11	PDB	2,262.00
31-01	DRDB	48.60			
31-01	Bank	923.40			
05-03	**Bank***	**888.00**			
05-03	**Bank ***	**277.20**			

**The reference here to Bank is to the Bank column in the Cash Book, as it is also in the Payables Ledger below.*

The two payments could be recorded in the Payables Ledger Control Account as one figure of £1,165.20, but it is better storytelling to do it in two transactions, as having separate transactions listed can help if it is necessary to track down potential errors. This would happen automatically in computerised accounting software, as the payments must be matched against specific transactions for specific suppliers.

Payables Ledger

SuperSuspension (SUP001)					
Debit £					Credit £
14-01	**PRDB**	**4.80**	10-11	PDB	282.00
05-03	**Bank**	**277.20**			

WonderWheels (WON001)					
Debit £					Credit £
15-01	**PRDB**	**12.00**	08-11	PDB	900.00
05-03	**Bank**	**888.00**			

The supplier accounts, if balanced, would now both show a balance of £0.00, as the invoices have been paid in full.

The totals in the Cash Book have not yet been added up, as there may be more transactions still to come.

Morgan is now going to pay some wages for two full-time employees, on March 11th.

Cash Book – Credit £							
Date	**Details**	**Cash**	**Bank**	**Trade Payables**	**VAT**	**Cash purchases**	**Other Expenses**
05-03	Super Suspension		888.00	888.00			
05-03	WonderWheels		277.20	277.20			
11-03	**Wages**		**3,160.00**				**3,160.00**
			TOTALS:				

These will require the following entry in the General Ledger:

Wages (7000)			
Debit £			Credit £
05-03	**Bank**	**3,160.00**	

Wages is an expense account, so it normally has debit entries. Expense accounts often have codes in the 7000 range, as in this case. The credit side of this transaction has already taken place in the Bank column on the credit side of the Cash Book.

An employee's wages are not subject to VAT, so no entry in the VAT column is required.

In computerised accounting, there are a range of different nominal codes, which you are not required to know, that could be used for wages to cover a range of wage types (casual staff, contractors, employees, net wages, director pay, etc.).

The next two transactions cover the payment of insurance and rent. Insurance is not subject to VAT, and rent is only subject to VAT in particular circumstances, which are not applicable here. Both payments are on March 13th.

Cash Book – Credit £							
Date	**Details**	**Cash**	**Bank**	**Trade Payables**	**VAT**	**Cash purchases**	**Other Expenses**
05-03	Super Suspension		888.00	888.00			
05-03	WonderWheels		277.20	277.20			
11-03	Wages		3,160.00				3,160.00
13-03	**Insurance**		**1,200.00**				**1,200.00**
13-03	**Rent**		**3,000.00**				**3,000.00**
			TOTALS:				

These will require the following entries in the General Ledger:

Insurance (7104)			
Debit £			Credit £
05-03	**Bank**	**1,200.00**	

Rent Paid (7100)			
Debit £			Credit £
05-03	**Bank**	**3,000.00**	

Both insurance and rent are expenses, and therefore require a debit entry to record the expense, and a nominal code in the 7000 range, although the exact number is not necessarily important. The credit side of these entries is in the Bank column on the credit side of the Cash Book.

Many business bank accounts have an applicable monthly charge, and Morgan's account for Delta Q Bikes Ltd is no exception, with a £10 monthly charge payable on the 15th of every month from March onwards.

Cash Book – Credit £							
Date	**Details**	**Cash**	**Bank**	**Trade Payables**	**VAT**	**Cash purchases**	**Other Expenses**
05-03	Super Suspension		888.00	888.00			
05-03	WonderWheels		277.20	277.20			
11-03	Wages		3,160.00				3,160.00
13-03	Insurance		1,200.00				1,200.00
13-03	Rent		3,000.00				3,000.00
15-03	**Bank Charges**		**10.00**				**10.00**
			TOTALS:				

Morgan is going to take drawings out of the business. Drawings (money taken out by the owner) are the opposite of Capital (money put in by the owner). This transaction involves £2,500 being taken out of the business bank account in cash. However, Morgan wants to have some cash available within the business, so she withdraws £3,000 – taking £2500 for herself and £500 to remain within the business. This is done on March 18th.

There is one final transaction as well, the impact of which will be seen in the next chapter. Out of the £500 cash withdrawn for use in the business, £200 of that will be transferred to petty cash.

At this stage, only half of the transaction will be shown, a credit of £200 in the Cash column. The debit half of the transaction will be shown in chapter 6, which looks at the Petty Cash Book.

Cash Book – Credit £							
Date	**Details**	**Cash**	**Bank**	**Trade Payables**	**VAT**	**Cash purchases**	**Other Expenses**
05-03	Super Suspension		888.00	888.00			
05-03	WonderWheels		277.20	277.20			
11-03	Wages		3,160.00				3,160.00
13-03	Insurance		1,200.00				1,200.00
13-03	Rent		3,000.00				3,000.00
15-03	Bank Charges		10.00				10.00
18-03	**Drawings**		**2,500.00**				
18-03	**Contra**		**500.00**				
19-03	**Petty Cash**	**200.00**					
			TOTALS:	1,165.20			7,370.00

These transactions must be recorded separately in the bookkeeping, as they are for different purposes. The withdrawal of drawings is recorded in the General Ledger as follows:

Drawings (3010)			
Debit £			Credit £
18-03	**Bank**	**2,500.00**	

The cash withdrawal is a more complex entry, as it involves withdrawing cash from the bank (a credit entry in the bank column of the Cash Book) into cash (a debit entry in the cash column of the Cash Book).

This type of entry, with cash being withdrawn from or deposited into the bank, in conjunction with using a Cash Book, is known as a **contra** entry. Contra means between.

The presence of Contra in the details is an indicator to the bookkeeper that this credit entry in the Cash Book (in this case, in the Bank column) will have a matching debit entry in the Cash Book (in the Cash column).

Effectively, cash is being withdrawn (credit) from the Bank and deposited (debit) to Cash. The debit side of the transaction will be seen in the next part of the chapter, which considers receipts into the Cash Book.

The credit side of the bank in the Cash Book is now complete, and there are no cash entries at this stage. The Cash Book totals can be added up and entered, which can be seen above, although it is not yet possible to balance the account, as the receipts have not been entered.

Neither the drawings nor the contra entry are strictly speaking an expense, so there would be no need to put them in an analysed column.

Cash Book Receipts

For recording cash & bank receipts in the Cash Book, and for transferring those receipts to the General Ledger, there are two important points to note:

1. The entries in the Cash and Bank columns are complete, and form one half of the double-entry transaction.
2. The entries in the analysed columns are not double-entry and will form the second half of the double-entry transaction once transferred into the General Ledger.

This is because here the Cash Book is both a book of prime entry (analysed columns) and double-entry (Cash & Bank columns).

For analysed columns on the debit side of the Cash Book, the relevant double-entry must take place on the credit side of the account. This is because the debit part of the transaction is recorded in the Cash or Bank column.

For Delta Q Bikes Ltd, the following credit receipts from customers are outstanding:

Account	Debit £	Credit £
Westernpool Cycles	618.00	

This is received on March 2nd, with the following entry in the Cash Book:

Cash Book – Debit £							
Date	**Details**	**Cash**	**Bank**	**Trade Receivables**	**VAT**	**Cash Sales**	**Other Income**
01-03	Balance b/d		17,331.60				
02-03	Westernpool Cycles		618.00	618.00			
			TOTALS:				

Note that there is a balance brought down at the beginning of March on the debit side of the Cash Book in the Bank column, as this signifies how much money was in the bank on that date.

There is no entry in the VAT column, as VAT was recorded at the time of sale.

This will require the following transactions in the Receivables Ledger Control Account and the Receivables Ledger:

General Ledger

Receivables Ledger Control Account (2110)					
Debit £					Credit £
31-01	SDB	2550.00	08-02	Bank	1,755.00
			28-02	SRDB	132.00
			28-02	DRDB	45.00
			02-03	**Bank ***	**618.00**

**The reference here to Bank is to the Bank column in the Cash Book, as it is also in the Receivables Ledger below:*

If the account were balanced, it would show a balance of £0.00 as no money is owed by credit customers.

Receivables Ledger

Westernpool Cycles (WES001)					
Debit £					Credit £
04-02	SDB	750.00	07-02	SRDB	132.00
			02-03	**Bank**	**618.00**

The customer accounts, if balanced, would also now both show a balance of £0.00, as the invoices have been paid in full.

The totals in the Cash Book have not yet been added up, as there may be more transactions still to come.

Delta Q Bikes Ltd have now also made some online sales via their website, which need recording in the Cash Book and in the double-entry bookkeeping. They use a payment provider which processes the money from customers and pays them once a week.

There are two transactions to be entered. The first is for March 8th for £1,275.00 + VAT, the second is for March 15th for £983.00 + VAT.

Cash Book – Debit £

Date	Details	Cash	Bank	Trade Receivables	VAT	Cash Sales	Other Income
01-03	Balance b/d		17,331.60				
02-03	Westernpool Cycles		618.00	618.00			
08-03	**Online sales**		**1,530.00**		**255.00**	**1,275.00**	
15-03	**Online sales**		**1,179.60**		**196.60**	**983.00**	
			TOTALS:				

Transactions that include VAT, for which VAT has not yet been recorded (a cash sale or purchase), must be recorded in a particular way.

In the case of these online sales, the net amounts are recorded in the analysed Cash Sales column in the Cash Book, and the VAT amount is recorded in the analysed VAT column. This ensures that the correct amounts are recorded in the correct General Ledger account.

The whole amount (gross) received from the customers is recorded in the relevant Cash or Bank column. In this case, the money received was paid into the bank of Delta Q Bikes Ltd. Therefore, it is recorded in the Bank column.

At this point, it would be understandable for students to be confused and to put the amount received into the Cash column, as this is a Cash Sale. However:

- The Cash column refers to notes and coins.
- The analysed Cash Sales column refers to whether the transaction was buy now pay later or buy now pay now, NOT the method of payment.

Students also often confuse the two columns by putting the net amount in the Cash or Bank column and the gross amount in the analysed column.

We have already seen in chapter 4 that the business has a General Ledger account called Sales – Shops, with a nominal code of 4000. The business has decided that it wants to be able to record sales to shops and online sales separately so that these transactions will be entered into the General Ledger under a different code.

Sales – Online Account (4001)

Debit £				Credit £
		08-03	**Bank**	**1,275.00**
		15-03	**Bank**	**983.00**

The entries in the Sales – Online Account are entered on the credit side of the account. This is because this is an income account, which normally has credit entries, and the debit side of the transaction has already been recorded in the Bank column of the Cash Book. Only the net amount is recorded in the income account.

As another option, they could be recorded in a Cash Sales Account in the General Ledger.

There is VAT on these two transactions, so the VAT must also be recorded.

VAT Account (2200)					
Debit £					Credit £
01-01	Bank	2,500.00	31-01	PRDB	20.80
01-01	Bank	2,250.00	31-01	DRDB	8.10
31-01	PDB	377.00	31-01	Balance c/d	5,098.10
		5,127.00			5,127.00
01-02	Balance b/d	5,098.10	28-02	SDB	425.00
28-02	SRDB	22.00	28-02	Balance c/d	4,702.60
28-02	DADB	7.50			
		5,127.60			5,127.60
01-03	Balance b/d	4,702.60	**08-03**	**Bank**	**255.00**
			15-03	**Bank**	**196.60**

The VAT Account shown here is certainly more complex than students will normally see in activities and assessments, although seeing the transactions in context over a three-month period, complete with monthly balancing, enables students to see how the balance of an account changes over time, with examples of the balancing process in action.

In a manual accounting system, the VAT total may be added in one transaction from a subtotalled column in the Cash Book, using the figure of £451.60. For computerised accounting software, each transaction will be recorded separately, which is preferred. In many assessment activities, the subtotalled figure will be the one that is added to the account, and this will be seen in some activities at the end of this chapter.

Morgan is fortunate that the bank that she chose for Delta Q Bikes Ltd pays interest on deposits, and so this month the business has received some interest that should be recorded in the Cash Book. This is for £1.50, received on March 16th.

Cash Book – Debit £							
Date	**Details**	**Cash**	**Bank**	**Trade Receivables**	**VAT**	**Cash Sales**	**Other Income**
01-03	Balance b/d		17,331.60				
02-03	Westernpool Cycles		618.00	618.00			
08-03	Online sales		1,530.00		255.00	1,275.00	
15-03	Online sales		1,179.60		196.60	983.00	
16-03	**Bank Interest Received**		**1.50**				1.50
			TOTALS:				

Bank Interest Received is classed as income, so Other Income is the most appropriate analysed column. VAT is not applicable for such income, so the whole amount is recorded in both the Bank and Other Income columns before being recorded in the General Ledger.

Bank Interest Received (4900)			
Debit £			Credit £
	16-03	**Bank**	**1.50**

It has previously been discussed that the 4000 range is the nominal code range for Sales and related accounts. It is also often used as the code range for miscellaneous forms of income.

The next transaction to be recorded on the debit side of the Cash Book is one for which we have already seen the credit component. This was the withdrawal of £500 of cash on March 18th, which was a contra entry. The word contra means between, as this money was moved between the Bank column (credit bank, as it was withdrawn) and the Cash column (debit Cash, as it was deposited to cash).

Cash Book – Debit £							
Date	**Details**	**Cash**	**Bank**	**Trade Receivables**	**VAT**	**Cash Sales**	**Other Income**
01-03	Balance b/d		17,331.60				
02-03	Westernpool Cycles		618.00	618.00			
08-03	Online sales		1,530.00		255.00	1,275.00	
15-03	Online sales		1,179.60		196.60	983.00	
16-03	Bank Interest Received		1.50				1.50
18-03	**Contra**	**500.00**					
			TOTALS:				

All payments and receipts have been made, so now it is time to look at both sides of the Cash Book together. It has not yet been balanced, but the columns are now totalled. The Cash Book will be balanced on the next page.

Cash Book – Debit £

Date	Details	Cash	Bank	Trade Receivables	VAT	Cash Sales	Other Income
01-03	Balance b/d		17,331.60				
02-03	Westernpool Cycles		618.00	618.00			
08-03	Online sales		1,530.00		255.00	1,275.00	
15-03	Online sales		1,179.60		196.60	983.00	
16-03	Bank Interest Received		1.50				1.50
18-03	Contra	500.00					
			TOTALS:	618.00	451.60	2,258.00	1.50

Cash Book – Credit £

Date	Details	Cash	Bank	Trade Payables	VAT	Cash purchases	Other Expenses
05-03	Super Suspension		888.00	888.00			
05-03	WonderWheels		277.20	277.20			
11-03	Wages		3,160.00				3,160.00
13-03	Insurance		1,200.00				1,200.00
13-03	Rent		3,000.00				3,000.00
15-03	Bank Charges		10.00				10.00
18-03	Drawings		2,500.00				
18-03	Contra		500.00				
19-03	Petty Cash	200.00					
			TOTALS:	1,165.20			7,370.00

Balancing the Cash Book

The Cash and Bank columns must be balanced separately, as they are different balances. In this case, they will be balanced on March 19th, as we still have petty cash transactions to deal with in the next chapter. The balanced Cash Book is shown on the next page.

Cash Book – Debit £							
Date	**Details**	**Cash**	**Bank**	**Trade Receivables**	**VAT**	**Cash Sales**	**Other Income**
01-03	Balance b/d		17,331.60				
02-03	Westernpool Cycles		618.00	618.00			
08-03	Online sales		1,530.00		255.00	1,275.00	
15-03	Online sales		1,179.60		196.60	983.00	
16-03	Bank Interest Received		1.50				1.50
18-03	Contra	500.00					
		500.00	20,660.70				
19-03	Balance b/d	300.00	9,125.50				
			TOTALS:	618.00	451.60	2,258.00	1.50

Cash Book – Credit £							
Date	**Details**	**Cash**	**Bank**	**Trade Payables**	**VAT**	**Cash purchases**	**Other Expenses**
05-03	Super Suspension		888.00	888.00			
05-03	WonderWheels		277.20	277.20			
11-03	Wages		3,160.00				3,160.00
13-03	Insurance		1,200.00				1,200.00
13-03	Rent		3,000.00				3,000.00
15-03	Bank Charges		10.00				10.00
18-03	Drawings		2,500.00				
18-03	Contra		500.00				
19-03	Petty Cash	200.00					
19-03	Balance c/d	300.00	9,125.50				
		500.00	20,660.70				
			TOTALS:	1,165.20			7,370.00

The Cash column has a balance brought down of £300.00.

This is because of:

- A withdrawal of £500.00 of cash from the bank that was deposited into cash.
- A transfer of £200 of cash into petty cash.

Cash can only ever have a balance brought down on the debit side (the actual balance of cash) and a balance carried down on the credit side. This is because it is not possible to have negative cash. Although a bank account can be overdrawn, this is not the case with cash. As long as the business has some, cash is always an asset with a debit balance.

The Bank column has a balance brought down of £9,125.50.

This is because of:

- An opening debit balance of £17,331.60.
- Payments/drawings/transfers on the credit side of the Cash Book of £11,535.20.
- Receipts on the debit side of the Cash Book of £3,329.10.

The business continues to have a debit balance, indicating money in the bank. The balance brought down and carried down in the Bank column of the Cash Book can be on either side of the account, depending on whether the business has money in the bank, or is overdrawn and has a liability to the bank.

The two columns, Cash and Bank, must always be balanced separately, as they are recording different elements of the business.

A business may choose to have, rather than using the Cash and Book columns of the Cash Book as double-entry, separate Cash and Bank Control Accounts.

In this case, the opening and closing balances would be recorded in the relevant control account, as well as a summary of payments and receipts.

Sources of Information

When entering transactions into the Cash Book, there may be a wide range of information sources, including:

- Online banking (direct debits, standing orders).
- Remittance advices (either from customers or from the business itself when paying suppliers).
- Paying-in slips (for when money is paid into the bank).
- Cheque stubs (for when cheques are sent to suppliers and for other purchases).
- Cash receipts (given when purchasing items).

Students need to be aware of the careful use of the word receipt. For example, a business may make a payment for an item yet receive a cash receipt (a document from the seller, confirming the sale). Here, a receipt is the name of the document received, which is like an invoice and is not an indication that money has been received.

Recurring Items

A business such as Delta Q Bikes Ltd may have several transactions that can be identified as **recurring items**, known in some accounting software as **recurring entries**.

Recurring items are usually items that are regular payments, although depending on the business they can also be receipts.

Examples of Delta Q Bikes Ltd transactions that could be recurring items include:

- Rent
- Insurance
- Bank Loan (although no payments have yet been made on the bank loan)

Bank charges could also be set up as a recurring item, although its usefulness would depend on the extent to which the charges are the same every month.

Recurring items are usually those payments (or receipts) that stay static for some time, so a year's worth of insurance with 12 identical monthly payments on the same date, or a year's rent with 12 identical monthly payments on the same date, are ideal candidates.

Utility bills such as water, electricity or gas are also suitable candidates if they are a regular fixed direct debit or standing order (students will study these payment methods more in the next unit). Variable utility bills would not be appropriate as recurring items.

Most accounting software has a facility for adding recurring items. It is usually a case of setting up the relevant payment from the bank in the software, and then setting it up as a recurring item. This will normally involve setting up the date (for example, the 13th of the month) and the transaction frequency (for example, monthly).

This automation of recurring items can help minimise the amount of work required to enter certain transactions, as well as budgeting and reporting for expected upcoming costs using the bookkeeping records of the business.

Cash and Bank Control Accounts

Rather than operating the Cash Book as a book of prime entry and double-entry bookkeeping, a business may instead have a Cash and Bank Control Account.

In this case, a summary of payments and receipts would be added to the account at the end of the week or month, which is appropriate for the business.

In a Cash Control Account for Delta Q Bikes Ltd, it would look like this: (for March)

Cash Control Account (1210)					
Debit £					**Credit £**
19-03	CB	500.00	19-03	CB	200.00
			19-03	Balance c/d	300.00
		500.00			500.00
19-03	Balance b/d	300.00			

In this case, CB refers to the Cash Book, from where the information came.

In a Bank Control Account for Delta Q Bikes Ltd, it would look like this: (for March)

Bank Control Account (1200)					
Debit *(dr)*		**£**	**Credit *(cr)***		**£**
01-03	Balance b/d	17,331.60	19-03	CB	11,535.20
19-03	CB	3.329.10	19-03	Balance c/d	9,125.50
		20,660.70			20,660.70
19-03	Balance b/d	9,125.50			

This process will not be used in a computerised accounting system.

Account Balances

At the end of chapter 4, we had the following trial balance, indicating the balance of individual accounts in the General Ledger at that time:

Trial Balance Delta Q Bikes Ltd February 28th			
Nominal Code	Account	Debit £	Credit £
0010	Machinery – At Cost	12,500.00	
1200	Bank	17,331.60	
2100	Payables Ledger Control Account		1,165.20
2110	Receivables Ledger Control Account	618.00	
2200	VAT	4,702.60	
2500	Bank Loan		25,000.00
3000	Capital		20,000.00
4000	Sales - Shops		2,125.00
4009	Discounts Allowed	37.50	
4050	Sales Returns	110.00	
5000	Purchases – Raw Materials	13,135.00	
5009	Discounts Received		40.50
5050	Purchases Returns		104.00
	Total	48,434.70	48,434.70

Various transactions have taken place in the Cash Book and the General Ledger during the month of March, which means that the Trial Balance has changed.

The Payables Ledger Control Account and the Receivables Ledger Control Account will not be shown in the list of balances making up the trial balance at the end of March. This is because all suppliers have been paid, and all customers have paid, so those account balances are zero. Only accounts for which there is a balance are normally shown in the trial balance, as otherwise it would be unnecessarily long and unwieldy to read.

Although it has not been seen in this chapter previously, the nominal code 1210 has been assigned to Cash.

The trial balance was extracted on March 19th, not the end of the month, to show the petty cash transaction on that date, and petty cash has been assigned the code 1230.

Trial Balance Delta Q Bikes Ltd March 19th			
Nominal Code	**Account**	**Debit £**	**Credit £**
0010	Machinery – At Cost	12,500.00	
1200	**Bank**	**9,125.50**	
1210	**Cash**	**300.00**	
1230	**Petty Cash**	**200.00**	
2200	**VAT**	**4,251.00**	
2500	Bank Loan		25,000.00
3000	Capital		20,000.00
3010	**Drawings**	**2,500.00**	
4000	Sales - Shops		2,125.00
4001	**Sales - Online**		**2,258.00**
4009	Discounts Allowed	37.50	
4050	Sales Returns	110.00	
4900	**Bank Interest Received**		**1.50**
5000	Purchases – Raw Materials	13,135.00	
5009	Discounts Received		40.50
5050	Purchases Returns		104.00
7000	**Wages**	**3,160.00**	
7100	**Rent Paid**	**3,000.00**	
7104	**Insurance**	**1,200.00**	
7901	**Bank Charges**	**10.00**	
	Total	**49,529.00**	**49,529.00**

This trial balance now shows a much wider range of asset categories:

- Assets
- Liabilities
- Sales
- Purchases
- Expenses

The Bank Account and the VAT Account are both assets as they have debit balances, indicating either money owned (in the case of the Bank Account) or money owed (in the case of the VAT Account.

The changes in the trial balance are because of the following transactions that have taken place in this chapter, covering:

- Payments or withdrawals in the Cash Book
- Receipts or deposits in the Cash Book

References to Cash or Bank are to the Cash and Bank columns in the Cash Book.

Account	Debit £	Credit £
Payables Ledger Control Account	888.00	
Bank		888.00
Payables Ledger Control Account	277.20	
Bank		277.20
Wages	3,160.00	
Bank		3,160.00
Insurance	1,200.00	
Bank		1,200.00
Rent Paid	3000.00	
Bank		3,000.00
Bank Charges	10.00	
Bank		10.00
Drawings	2,500.00	
Bank		2,500.00
Bank		500.00
Cash	500.00	
Cash		200.00
Petty Cash	200.00	
Bank	618.00	
Receivables Ledger Control Account		618.00
Bank	1,530.00	
Sales - Online		1,275.00
VAT		255.00
Bank	1,179.60	
Sales - Online		983.00
VAT		196.60
Bank	1.50	
Bank Interest Received		1.50

In each case, the Bank and Cash columns follow Rule 1 of double-entry, and the other accounts follow Rule 2, as explained earlier in the book.

Digital Focus

Students should practice the following skills in computerised accounting software.

1. Recording payments received from customers.
2. Recording payments made to suppliers.
3. Allocating payments made or received against supplier & customer accounts.
4. Recording payments for cash purchases or expenses.
5. Recording receipts for cash sales or income.

This can most easily be done by entering the transactions that are listed in this chapter, using the supplier and customer accounts set up in earlier chapters, and setting up nominal codes as necessary for expenses and income.

The most complicated of the tasks is probably task 3, allocating payments against opening balances, or in the case of this scenario, particular invoices, credit notes or prompt payments. Credit notes will need to be created on the system for the amount of the PPD discount in both cases, although this may have been done already in chapters 3 and 4.

Students should also practice generating or exporting an Audit Trail. This document shows all the transactions that have been entered, and accounting software can often show a summary or a detailed version. The detailed version will usually give a clearer account of the double-entry that is taking place.

Students could also practice generating a statement of account for a customer, looking at customer and supplier activity to see what has happened in transactions so far.

Students will need to be wary about entering VAT. Accounting software will often make presumptions about VAT that may or may not be correct, so students need to ensure that the accounting software only adds VAT when required.

Most accounting software is unlikely to treat cash and bank transactions in the form of the Cash Book that has been seen in this chapter, although some software will. Bank & cash transactions are usually treated as separate General Ledger accounts.

Summary

The Cash Book is a book of prime entry and double-entry for the recording of cash (excluding petty cash) and bank transactions in the business.

A cash book will have columns on both the debit and credit sides for recording money in and out. These two columns are the double-entry record for cash (notes and coins) and the bank.

A cash book may also have a number of analysed columns, both on the debit and credit side. These are for recording different categories of expenses and income, as well as money paid to credit suppliers and received from credit customers. These analysed columns are not double-entry, and the figures entered in these columns must be transferred to the double-entry bookkeeping system to the correct accounts.

VAT need not be recorded in the Cash Book concerning the payment made to a supplier or payment received from a customer. This is because the VAT was already recorded under accruals accounting at the time of sale or purchase.

For cash purchases or cash sales, VAT will need to be recorded in the Cash Book. The VAT amount will be recorded in the analysed VAT column, the net amount will be recorded in the relevant analysed expense, income, purchase or sale column, and the gross (net plus VAT) will be recorded in the Cash or Bank column, as the full amount of money that has changed hands.

If a customer pays by a combination of bank transfer/cheque/cash, the sums must be recorded in the correct Cash or Bank columns accordingly.

A contra entry is recorded when cash is taken out of the bank but remains as cash in the business, or when cash previously received and recorded in the Cash column is subsequently deposited to the bank. Petty cash is recorded separately.

As with other General Ledger accounts, the Cash and Bank columns (which are double-entry) must be balanced. These must be balanced separately rather than together, as they are about different sums.

Businesses that do not have a Cash Book may use a Cash Control Account or a Bank Control Account to record a summary of the payments made or sums received during a particular period.

Accounting software rarely uses the Cash Book method, and it is more likely to have separate Cash and Bank Accounts in the General Ledger into which all transactions are recorded.

Skills & Knowledge Test – Chapter 5

QUESTION 35

A credit customer has just paid an invoice for £200 + VAT by bank transfer. What will be the correct entry in the Cash Book?

Credit the Bank column with £240, enter £240 in the Trade Receivables column, no entry in the VAT column.	
Credit the Bank column with £240, enter £200 in the Trade Receivables column, enter £40 in the VAT column.	
Debit the Bank column with £240, enter £240 in the Trade Receivables column, no entry in the VAT column.	
Debit the Bank column with £240, enter £200 in the Trade Receivables column, enter £40 in the VAT column.	

QUESTION 36

A credit supplier has just been paid £400 + VAT by bank transfer. What will be the correct entry in the Cash Book?

Credit the Bank column with £480, enter £480 in the Trade Payables column, no entry in the VAT column.	
Credit the Bank column with £480, enter £400 in the Trade Receivables column, enter £80 in the VAT column.	
Debit the Bank column with £480, enter £480 in the Trade Receivables column, no entry in the VAT column.	
Debit the Bank column with £480, enter £400 in the Trade Receivables column, enter £80 in the VAT column.	

QUESTION 37

You have made cash sales (in cash) of £150 + VAT in cash. What will be the correct entry in the Cash Book?

Debit the Cash column with £180, enter £150 in the Cash Sales column and £30 in the VAT column.	
Debit the Cash column with £180, enter £180 in the Cash Sales column, no entry in the VAT column.	
Credit the Cash column with £180, enter £150 in the Cash Sales column and £30 in the VAT column.	
Credit the Cash column with £180, enter £180 in the Cash Sales column, no entry in the VAT column.	

QUESTION 38

You have made cash purchases of £60 + VAT in cash. What will be the correct entry in the Cash Book?

Debit the Bank column with £60, enter £60 in the Cash Purchases column, no entry in the VAT column	
Credit the Bank column with £72, enter £60 in the Cash Purchases column and £12 in the VAT column	
Credit the Cash column with £72, enter £60 in the Cash Purchases column and £12 in the VAT column	
Credit the Cash column with £60, enter £60 in the Cash Purchases column, no entry in the VAT column	

QUESTION 39

Indicate for the following statements whether they are true or false.

	True	False
The Bank column of the Cash Book can be carried down on either side, depending on the balance.		
The Cash column of the Cash Book can be carried down on either side, depending on the balance.		

QUESTION 40

The following items need to be added to the debit side of the Cash Book. Add them and then complete the Cash Book as appropriate and total each column.

£210 including VAT received from a credit customer, Company A, by bank transfer.

£300 including VAT received. This is £225 by cheque, £75 in cash for goods received today from Company B.

Cash Book

Details	Cash	Bank	VAT	Trade Receivables	Cash Sales
Balance b/d	276	1,456			
Company A					
Company B					
Totals					

The credit side of the cash book for the same period shows that there were payments of cash of £108. What is the cash balance?

The credit side of the Cash Book for the same period shows that there were payments from the bank of £283. What is the bank account balance?

Is the bank balance a debit or a credit balance in the Cash Book?

Debit	Credit

QUESTION 41

These are Cash Book totals for the end of the time period.

Cash £	Bank £	VAT £	Trade Receivables £	Cash Sales £	Cash £	Bank £	VAT £		Trade Payables £	Cash Purchases £
416	15881	----	983	----	614	15881	108		392	113

What will be the entries in the General Ledger?

Account	**Amount £**	**Debit**	**Credit**

QUESTION 42

Indicate whether the following payments or receipts will be recorded on the credit or debit side of the Cash Book.

Transaction	**Debit**	**Credit**
Payment to credit supplier		
Payment from credit customer		
Bank interest received		
Bank charges paid		
Cash sales		
Cash purchases		
VAT on sales		
VAT on purchases		

QUESTION 43

Indicate whether the following payments or receipts will be recorded in the Cash or Bank column of the Cash Book.

Transaction	Cash	Bank
A credit customer pays you in cash		
A credit supplier is paid by cheque		
A cash purchase paid by debit card		
A cash sale paid by cheque		
Cash received for a cash sale		

This section has been created for you should you wish to use it to make notes or for calculations.

The Petty Cash Book

Introduction

Before looking at the Petty Cash Book and seeing how transactions in this case study are applied to it, let us remind ourselves of the scenario for this unit.

Scenario
Morgan has started a business making and selling bicycles. This business is called Delta Q Bikes Ltd and makes both standard and electric bicycles. Bicycles are sold to shops, who then sell them on to customers, and are also sold direct to customers by Delta Q Bikes Ltd via their online shop and website. Morgan has put some of her own money into the business (this is known as capital) as well as money from a friend and a bank loan (which are known as liabilities). She has rented a property from which to manufacture bikes and store them in a warehouse and has hired two other employees. Morgan has also invested in specialist machinery (an asset) for manufacturing the bikes. The business will use a double-entry bookkeeping system, which uses a series of day books (for credit sales and purchases) linked to a Receivables Ledger, a Payables Ledger, and the General Ledger. The business will buy components and other items from suppliers, which are known as credit purchases, and will sell finished goods to shops, which are known as credit sales. Cash sales to retail customers, from the online website, are also recorded. A Cash Book and Petty Cash Book are used, both of which are books of prime entry and double-entry, and will record the money element of all purchases, expenses and income, as well as any drawings made by the owner.

The Petty Cash Book behaves in a very similar manner to the Cash Book, in that it is both a book of prime entry and double-entry, in this case for small cash (notes and coins) transactions only.

There are three main differences between the Petty Cash Book and the Cash Book:

- It only deals with cash (notes and coins), so there is no need for Cash and Bank columns. There is instead a single Amount column.
- It deals mostly with payments, although receipts are possible, particularly when it is being topped up.
- It often has a system for topping up at regular intervals.

In a larger business or financial department, there may be a Petty Cashier who has the prime responsibility for the Petty Cash Book.

Petty Cash Book

In a manual accounting system, the Petty Cash Book may typically be laid out in the following manner: (note that the credit side is wider and larger than the debit side)

Petty Cash Book								
Date	Details	Amount	Date	Details	Amount	VAT	Stationery	Other Expenses
				Totals:				

In an assessment, you are more likely to see a Petty Cash Book that contains only a credit side, as you are likely to be dealing with payments only, although a debit side is also necessary for topping up the amounts.

There was one petty cash transaction in Delta Q Bikes Ltd, a transfer of £200.00 into petty cash on March 19th, on the credit side of the Cash Book in chapter 5. Therefore, the Petty Cash Book for Delta Q Bikes Ltd currently looks like this:

Petty Cash Book								
Date	Details	Amount	Date	Details	Amount	VAT	Stationery	Other Expenses
19-03	**Cash**	**200.00**						
				Totals:				

Many businesses that use a Petty Cash Book or a similar system will follow what is known as the imprest system.

In an imprest system, the petty cash is topped to a set amount at the beginning of every time period, e.g., weekly or monthly, as appropriate.

Imprest System
A business starts the month with £100.00 in its Petty Cash Book. During the month, the business spends £75.50, leaving it with a balance of £24.50. At the end of the month, ready for the beginning of the next month, £75.50 is withdrawn from cash (in the Cash Book) and transferred into the Petty Cash Book to restore the balance of £100.00. The same procedure is followed at the end/beginning of every month. This is an imprest system.

In this case, the double-entry to restore the imprest would be:

Account	Debit £	Credit £
Petty Cash	75.50	
Cash		75.50

The exact process will vary, a business may:

- Withdraw the necessary amount from its cash reserves, which would require crediting cash, as above.
- Write a cheque, payable to 'Cash', and take it to the bank, giving them the correct amount in cash, which would then be added to the Petty Cash Book. In this case, the credit part of the transaction would be Bank rather than Cash.

Some businesses will use a non-imprest system. This is where the Petty Cash Book is topped up with irregular amounts and irregular intervals, often when the balance of the Petty Cash Book gets low.

It is more likely, although not certain, that larger businesses are more likely to use an imprest system, whereas smaller businesses are more likely to use a non-imprest system. It is entirely down to the business which they intend to do.

Morgan has decided that for clarity and ease, the business will follow an imprest system for petty cash transactions.

Delta Q Bikes Ltd will have a number of small payments during the rest of March, all of which will come from the Petty Cash Book.

- Travel costs
- Stationery
- Office expenses

The stationery expenses will be recorded in the analysed column called Stationery. In contrast, the other expenses will be in the analysed column called Other Expenses, as Morgan expects that most of the business petty cash costs will be stationery, with occasional other expenses.

There are several ways in which the money in petty cash is spent:

- An employee buys an item or items out of their own money and is then reimbursed (money given back to them) for that amount, on production of a receipt.
- An employee is given some money out of petty cash to buy an item or items, and returns with the item(s), a receipt providing an important paper trail, and the change from the transaction.

Businesses will vary as to which method(s) they use, but most will use petty cash vouchers as part of the authorisation process. Most employees will not just be able to spend petty cash as and when they wish, as the business will most likely have policies regarding how money is spent and who may spend it.

For each of the expenses, a petty cash voucher is created.

The petty cash voucher is an important part of the authorisation process. A petty cash voucher may look like this:

Petty Cash Voucher	**Voucher no:** 098 **Date:** 20/03/2022
Details:	**Amount £:**
Tea	12.00
Coffee	9.00
VAT	4.20
Total:	25.20
Signed:	C Cheshire
Authorised	M Rothby

In this transaction, Morgan has authorised an employee to go to the shop to buy tea and coffee for the office, and has reimbursed them with this petty cash voucher as the evidence.

- The signature is the person claiming the expense.
- The authorisation is the person agreeing that it is an allowable business expense that can be claimed, often a line manager or business owner.
- Petty cash vouchers should be accompanied by the documentation in relation to the original transaction, e.g., a receipt.

A petty cash voucher could be created on the computer as a usable template, but books of petty cash vouchers are also readily available in stationery shops, as are invoices and purchase orders.

In the Petty Cash Book, this transaction would be entered:

Petty Cash Book								
Date	Details	Amount £	Date	Details	Amount	VAT	Stationery	Other Expenses
19-03	Cash	200.00	20-03	**Office Expenses**	**25.20**	**4.20**		**21.00**
				Totals:				

This transaction is very similar to transactions seen in the Cash Book in the previous chapter. There is a completed section for date and details, the gross total is in the Amount column (which replaces the Cash and Bank columns in the Cash Book), the VAT amount is in the VAT column and the net amount in the analysed expense column, in this case Other Expenses.

As with the Cash and Bank columns in the Cash Book, the Amount column in the Petty Cash Book fulfils the role of double-entry (so no other entry is required), whereas the analysed columns will require an entry to fulfil the other side of the double-entry transaction.

The transaction can then be entered into the double-entry bookkeeping in the General Ledger. In each case study, PCB refers to the Petty Cash Book and denotes that half of the double-entry transaction has already taken place there in the Amount column.

Office Expenses (7550)			
Debit £			Credit £
19-03	**PCB**	**21.00**	

The Office Expenses Account is an expense account, so a debit entry would be expected, and as with the Cash Book, an entry on the credit side of the analysed columns in the Petty Cash Book will be a debit entry in the relevant account in the General Ledger. The credit portion of the double-entry is already present in the Petty Cash Book in the Amount column.

VAT Account (2200)					
Debit £					Credit £
01-01	Bank	2,500.00	31-01	PRDB	20.80
01-01	Bank	2,250.00	31-01	DRDB	8.10
31-01	PDB	377.00	31-01	Balance c/d	5,098.10
		5,127.00			5,127.00
01-02	Balance b/d	5,098.10	28-02	SDB	425.00
28-02	SRDB	22.00	28-02	Balance c/d	4,702.60
28-02	DADB	7.50			
		5,127.60			5,127.60
01-03	Balance b/d	4,702.60	08-03	Bank	255.00
20-03	**PCB**	**4.20**	15-03	Bank	196.60

The VAT entry is on the debit side as it is taken from an analysed column in the Petty Cash Book, but also as the VAT spent on office expenses can be reclaimed from HMRC. The VAT entry here could be added as a total once all other entries have been made, which is the likely process in an assessment, and in activities at the end of this chapter. However, in this case, each entry is done separately, partly for better storytelling but also as it mirrors how this would be done in accounting software.

Morgan has also made a further transaction the next day from Petty Cash, going to the local stationery store and spending £42.50 (excluding VAT, but VAT is applicable) on stationery supplies.

Petty Cash Book								
Date	Details	Amount £	Date	Details	Amount	VAT	Stationery	Other Expenses
19-03	Cash	200.00	20-03	Office Expenses	25.20	4.20		21.00
			21-03	**Stationery**	**51.00**	**8.50**	**42.50**	
				Totals:				

Then the relevant transactions are entered into the General Ledger.

Stationery (7500)					
Debit £					Credit £
21-03	**PCB**	**42.50**			

As with Office Expenses, only the net amount is recorded in the Stationery account. This is the actual cost of the stationery as the VAT, which can be reclaimed from HMRC, is recorded in the VAT account.

VAT Account (2200)					
Debit £					Credit £
01-01	Bank	2,500.00	31-01	PRDB	20.80
01-01	Bank	2,250.00	31-01	DRDB	8.10
31-01	PDB	377.00	31-01	Balance c/d	5,098.10
		5,127.00			5,127.00
01-02	Balance b/d	5,098.10	28-02	SDB	425.00
28-02	SRDB	22.00	28-02	Balance c/d	4,702.60
28-02	DADB	7.50			
		5,127.60			5,127.60
01-03	Balance b/d	4,702.60	08-03	Bank	255.00
20-03	PCB	4.20	15-03	Bank	196.60
21-03	**PCB**	**8.50**			

Morgan now sends an employee on March 23rd to buy stamps in order to send out some business letters. Stamps are not subject to VAT. Morgan wants to buy £15.00 of stamps in total and wants to buy some of those stamps from the business, as she also has some personal letters to send, and being a busy owner of a new business has not had time to go to the Post Office herself.

In this case, the cost of the £15.00 of stamps bought by the business and the £5.00 of stamps sold by the business to Morgan must be recorded.

Petty Cash Book

Date	Details	Amount £	Date	Details	Amount	VAT	Stationery	Other Expenses
19-03	Cash	200.00	20-03	Office Expenses	25.20	4.20		21.00
23-03	**Stamps**	**5.00**	21-03	Stationery	51.00	8.50	42.50	
			23-03	**Stamps**	**15.00**			**15.00**
				Totals:				

For the bookkeeping to be accurate, it is important to record it as two transactions - a payment of £15.00 and a receipt of £5.00. So much of bookkeeping is, as the very first chapter of this book indicated, about being a faithful storyteller.

Postage (7501)

Debit £			Credit £		
23-03	**PCB**	**15.00**	**23-03**	**PCB**	**5.00**

This is the first example of a credit entry in an expense account. This is because the sale of £5.00 of stamps to Morgan in a personal capacity reduces the cost of the expense. The business is likely to (and should) provide a receipt to Morgan for this sale, so there is a paper trail. It would not be normal for the business to have a separate account in the General Ledger for Postages - Income, as it would not be considered to be real income but rather the reduction of an expense.

There is one more transaction to be considered here: Morgan took a train to a local and free conference for new business owners. The cost of the train was £47.50. Train travel is zero-rated (VAT is not charged on it, although technically it is charged at 0%). There is no column for train travel, so it is also placed in the analysed Other Expenses column. If Morgan had regular travel costs to record in the Petty Cash Book, it would be worth adding a column for Travel Costs. As VAT was irrelevant in this transaction, the gross amount is entered into the analysed Other Expenses column.

Petty Cash Book								
Date	Details	Amount £	Date	Details	Amount	VAT	Stationery	Other Expenses
19-03	Cash	200.00	20-03	Office Expenses	25.20	4.20		21.00
23-03	Stamps	5.00	21-03	Stationery	51.00	8.50	42.50	
			23-03	Stamps	15.00			15.00
			25-03	**Train Travel**	**47.50**			**47.50**
				Totals:				

The relevant entry is then made in the General Ledger, with no entry in the VAT Account.

Travel (7400)			
Debit £			Credit £
25-03	**PCB**	**47.50**	

As the payments are now complete, there is one final transaction before the Petty Cash Book can be balanced. Imprest needs to be restored.

The amount of imprest to be restored will always be:

The amount of expenses on the credit side **minus** any income on the debit side.

There have been expenses of £138.70 and income of £5.00. Therefore, the amount needed to restore the imprest is £133.70.

The imprest that has been restored here is by taking £133.70 out of the Cash of the business from the Cash Book and depositing it into the Petty Cash Book.

The double-entry for this would be:

Account	Debit £	Credit £
Petty Cash	133.70	
Cash		133.70

In the Petty Cash Book this would look like the following:

Petty Cash Book

Date	Details	Amount £	Date	Details	Amount	VAT	Stationery	Other Expenses
19-03	Cash	200.00	20-03	Office Expenses	25.20	4.20		21.00
23-03	Stamps	5.00	21-03	Stationery	51.00	8.50	42.50	
31-03	**Cash**	**133.70**	23-03	Stamps	15.00			15.00
			25-03	Train Travel	47.50			47.50
				Totals:				

It is easier and more helpful to restore the imprest before balancing the account. The Petty Cash Book can now be balanced. The subtotals have now been calculated, and, if not previously entered in the General Ledger, should now be entered. The sum of the analysed columns on the credit side (£138.70) should add up to the sum of the Amount column before balancing (£138.70). This is a useful check on the maths and correct placement of transactions and can flag up some errors.

Petty Cash Book

Date	Details	Amount £	Date	Details	Amount	VAT	Stationery	Other Expenses
19-03	Cash	200.00	20-03	Office Expenses	25.20	4.20		21.00
23-03	Stamps	5.00	21-03	Stationery	51.00	8.50	42.50	
31-03	Cash	133.70	23-03	Stamps	15.00			15.00
			25-03	Train Travel	47.50			47.50
			31-03	**Balance c/d**	**200.00**			
		338.70			**338.70**			
01-04	**Balance b/d**	**200.00**						
				Totals:		12.70	42.50	83.50

Astute students may have noticed that the amount of the balance carried down and the balance brought down are the same amount that the account is restored to at the beginning of the next period, £200.00. With a Petty Cash Book that uses the imprest system, this will always be the case, as long as the imprest is (correctly) restored before the account is balanced.

A common error that students make when restoring imprest is to, rather than restoring the imprest from the amount of expenses (plus any income), attempt to restore the imprest amount as the balance of the account.

For example, with an impress amount of £150, £90 has been spent during the month, leaving a balance of £60. A common error is to restore the imprest by adding £60, however this would only restore the balance to £120 rather than £150.

Withdrawing cash from the Cash Book also requires a Cash Book entry. For ease of viewing, the previous balancing of March 19th from chapter 5 will be removed, and the account will be balanced for March 31st. Restoring of imprest would not be added to an analysed column.

As with the Cash column of the Cash Book, there must be a balance brought down on the debit side of the Petty Cash Book, as there cannot be negative cash.

Cash Book – Debit £

Date	Details	Cash	Bank	Trade Receivables	VAT	Cash Sales	Other Income
01-03	Balance b/d		17,331.60				
02-03	Westernpool Cycles		618.00	618.00			
08-03	Online sales		1,530.00		255.00	1,275.00	
15-03	Online sales		1,179.60		196.60	983.00	
16-03	Bank Interest Received		1.50				1.50
18-03	Contra	500.00					
		500.00	20,660.70				
01-04	**Balance b/d**	**166.30**					
			TOTALS:	618.00	451.60	2,258.00	1.50

Cash Book – Credit £

Date	Details	Cash	Bank	Trade Payables	VAT	Cash purchases	Other Expenses
05-03	Super Suspension		888.00	888.00			
05-03	WonderWheels		277.20	277.20			
11-03	Wages		3160.00				3160.00
13-03	Insurance		1200.00				1200.00
13-03	Rent		3000.00				3000.00
15-03	Bank Charges		10.00				10.00
18-03	Drawings		2500.00				
18-03	Contra		500.00				
19-03	Petty Cash	200.00					
31-03	**Petty Cash Book**	**133.70**					
31-03	**Balance c/d**	**166.30**	9,125.50				
		500.00	20,660.70				
			TOTALS:	1,165.20			7,370.00

Petty Cash Reconciliation

When balancing the Petty Cash Book, it is important to check that the balance of the Petty Cash Book matches the amount of petty cash that is actually held by the business. This process is called **reconciliation**.

Ensuring that this process is as smooth as possible and that the amount of cash held is correct can be ensured by following procedures such as:

- Petty cash being kept in a locked and secure tin.
- Limited authorisation of access to petty cash.
- Regular balancing and reconciliation.
- Reimbursement of petty cash amounts spent, rather than giving money out ahead of the expenditure.
- Use of petty cash vouchers to confirm authorisation of expenditure.
- Insistence of receipts and other documentation for all petty cash purchase.

The following is an example of a Petty Cash reconciliation, not related to the case study in this book:

Petty Cash Book	**Date:** 08/08/2021
£50 notes	£0.00
£20 notes	£20.00
£10 notes	£20.00
£5 notes	£5.00
£2 coin	£4.00
£1 coin	£11.00
50p coin	£2.50
20p coin	£0.80
10p coin	£0.90
5p coin	£0.55
2p coin	£0.14
1p coin	£0.01
Balance of Petty Cash in hand £	64.90
Balance of Petty Cash Book £	64.90

The process involves counting all cash, recording the amounts/values of each note or coin held, and comparing those amounts with the amount recorded in the Petty Cash Book.

Any discrepancies should be immediately investigated. Potential errors include:

- Misappropriation (stealing) of petty cash funds.
- Miscounting of petty cash.
- Errors in recording of entries in the Petty Cash Book.

A common feature of bookkeeping and accounting, especially in larger businesses, is the division of labour with the finance function, but also the checking of each other's work.

If the Petty Cashier cannot reconcile the Petty Cash Book with actual cash in hand, a second person from within the business could be entrusted to do similar checks, as sometimes it is easier for other people to spot errors than ourselves.

Petty Cash Control Account

Instead of using the Petty Cash Book as both prime entry and double-entry bookkeeping, it may operate the Petty Cash Book as prime entry only, in which case, periodically at the end of the week or month, the sum of payments and receipts will be transferred to a Petty Cash Control Account. CB denotes the Cash Book, and PCB denotes the Petty Cash Book.

Petty Cash Control Account (1200)					
Debit *(dr)*		£	Credit *(cr)*		£
19-03	CB	200.00	19-03	PCB	138.70
31-03	PCB	5.00	31-03	Balance c/d	200.00
31-03	CB	133.70			
		338.70			338.70
01-04	Balance b/d	200.00			

Account Balances

At the end of chapter 5, we had the following trial balance, indicating the balance of individual accounts in the General Ledger at that time:

Trial Balance Delta Q Bikes Ltd March 19th			
Nominal Code	**Account**	**Debit £**	**Credit £**
0010	Machinery	12,500.00	
1200	Bank	9,125.50	
1210	Cash	300.00	
1230	Petty Cash	200.00	
2200	VAT	4,251.00	
2500	Bank Loan		25,000.00
3000	Capital		20,000.00
3010	Drawings	2,500.00	
4000	Sales - Shops		2,125.00
4001	Sales - Online		2,258.00
4009	Discounts Allowed	37.50	
4050	Sales Returns	110.00	
4900	Bank Interest Received		1.50
5000	Purchases	13,135.00	
5009	Discounts Received		40.50
5050	Purchases Returns		104.00
7000	Wages	3,160.00	
7100	Rent Paid	3,000.00	
7104	Insurance	1,200.00	
7901	Bank Charges	10.00	
	Total	49,529.00	49,529.00

A number of transactions have taken place in this chapter involving the Petty Cash Book, which means the trial balance at the end of March is as follows:

Trial Balance Delta Q Bikes Ltd March 31st			
Nominal Code	Account	Debit £	Credit £
0010	Machinery	12,500.00	
1200	Bank	9,125.50	
1210	**Cash**	**166.30**	
1230	**Petty Cash**	**200.00**	
2200	**VAT**	**4,263.70**	
2500	Bank Loan		25,000.00
3000	Capital		20,000.00
3010	Drawings	2,500.00	
4000	Sales - Shops		2,125.00
4001	Sales - Online		2,258.00
4009	Discounts Allowed	37.50	
4050	Sales Returns	110.00	
4900	Bank Interest Received		1.50
5000	Purchases	13,135.00	
5009	Discounts Received		40.50
5050	Purchases Returns		104.00
7000	Wages	3,160.00	
7100	Rent Paid	3,000.00	
7104	Insurance	1,200.00	
7400	**Travel**	**47.50**	
7500	**Stationery**	**42.50**	
7501	**Postage**	**10.00**	
7550	**Office Expenses**	**21.00**	
7901	Bank Charges	10.00	
	Total	**49,529.00**	**49,529.00**

Unusually, this trial balance does not involve a change in the overall totals at the bottom, just a change in individual balances.

This is because the only balances that change are debit balances, which involve increased or decreased cash or petty cash balances, increases to expense accounts, then finally an increase to the debit balance of the VAT Account.

Digital Focus

Students can practice the following skills:

- Entering petty cash payments
- Entering petty cash receipts
- Restoring the imprest
- Exporting or printing out a petty cash statement

Petty Cash can easily be managed within a computerised accounting system. Some software will already have an account for this purpose, whilst some software will need an account creating/setting up. For example, from the perspective of Sage (one manufacturer of accounting software), a Petty Cash Account can be set up as a type of 'Bank' account.

Within accounting software, petty cash is likely to be an account, rather than a combination, as in this chapter of prime entry and double-entry bookkeeping.

As all of the transactions in this scenario have now been completed, students should also practice generating or exporting an Audit Trail. This document shows all of the transactions that have been entered, and accounting software can often show a summary or a detailed version. The detailed version will usually give a clearer account of the double-entry that is taking place.

Students could also export or print out a final trial balance and compare their trial balance with the trial balance on the previous page.

The trial balance will be a significant part of the unit, Principles of Bookkeeping Controls, so familiarity with its layout, its process, and what accounts go on which side are useful preparations for that unit.

Accounting software often has the facility to reset data back to the beginning, with no transactions or account details listed. If this feature is available within the accounting software the student is using, they could reset their data or set the company up from the very beginning, and practice entering the transactions again, to increase familiarity with these important processes.

Summary

The Petty Cash Book is the main book of prime entry and double-entry bookkeeping for small value petty cash transactions.

Many businesses will operate the Petty Cash Book according to the imprest system. This system means that the Petty Cash Book is topped up to the same amount every week or month. The amount will vary from business to business according to their needs. Businesses may also use a non-imprest system, where the Petty Cash Book is topped up with irregular amounts.

The Amount column is the double-entry component of the Petty Cash Book, and the analysed columns are prime entry, which requires entries in the relevant General Ledger accounts. Analysed columns are named appropriate to the business and their needs.

Most entries in the Petty Cash Book are likely to be payments (with equivalent debit entries in General Ledger accounts). However, there will be some receipts, notably transfers into the Petty Cash Book in order to restore the imprest, and some small receipts when business items are sold for personal purposes, such as stamps.

The Petty Cash Book will always have a balance carried down on the credit side and a balance brought down on the debit side. This is because the business cannot have negative cash.

When the Petty Cash Book is balanced, it should be compared with the amount of petty cash within the business, a process called reconciliation. Discrepancies should be investigated, but policies and procedures can be implemented to minimise the number of problems and issues that occur.

Typical procedures will include keeping the petty cash securely out of the reach of those not authorised to access it, and only reimbursing amounts which follow the policies and procedures of the business.

Businesses will often use petty cash vouchers as part of the authorisation process. This ensures that only relevant and authorised petty cash expenses are processed.

Businesses that operate the Petty Cash Book as a book of prime entry only may use a Petty Cash Control account, into which a summary of debits and credits will entered at the end of every week or month as appropriate.

Skills & Knowledge Test – Chapter 6

QUESTION 44

Which of the following statements accurately describes the imprest system?

When the Petty Cash is topped up, it is always topped up to the same amount.	
When the Petty Cash is topped up, it is topped up to a different amount each time.	

QUESTION 45

All businesses use the imprest system, true or false?

True	False

QUESTION 46

The amount to which petty cash is topped up according to the imprest system may be set in company policies, true or false?

True	False

QUESTION 47

The Petty Cash Book began with an opening balance of £250.00. During the month there were payments of £132.87 and receipts of £11.00. What will be the double-entry required to restore the imprest from the Bank Account?

Account	**Amount £**	**Debit**	**Credit**

QUESTION 48

The Petty Cash Book began with an opening balance of £300.00. During the month there were payments of £192.16. What will be the double-entry required to restore the imprest from the cash held in the business?

Account	Amount £	Debit	Credit

QUESTION 49

The business restores its imprest to £200 on the first day of every month. These are the petty cash payments for one month.

Date	Details	Amount £	Date	Details	Amount £	VAT £	Office Supplies £	Travel £	Misc. expenses £
1 Nov	Bal b/d	200.00	4 Nov	Office	75.00	12.50	62.50		
				Travel	10.00			10.00	
				Misc.	66.00	11.00			55.00
				Travel	25.50			25.50	

What entry in the Petty Cash Book is required to restore the imprest from the bank?

Details	Amount £	Debit	Credit

What will be the total of the VAT column in the Petty Cash Book? The £ symbol is not required.

QUESTION 50

Enter the following transactions into the Petty Cash Book and total the columns:

- January 4th - Supplies for the office, £125.00 (excluding VAT)
- January 5th - Train travel, £18.90 (no VAT)
- January 6th - Train travel, £21.50 (no VAT)
- January 8th - Book purchase, £19.00 (no VAT)

Total the columns on the credit side of the Petty Cash Book once complete.

Date	Details	Amount £	Date	Details	Amount £	VAT £	Office Supplies £	Travel £	Cash purchases £
1 Jan	Bal b/d	300.00							
				Totals:					

Transfer the totals to the General Ledger.

Account	Amount £	Debit	Credit

What is the balance of the account (how much money is left in Petty Cash)? The £ symbol is not required.

This section has been created for you should you wish to use it to make notes or for calculations.

Assessment Support

Introduction

One of the most important points to remember about AAT assessments is that they are professional qualifications for a professional organisation. As the AAT is a professional organisation preparing students for a profession with necessarily exacting standards, this integrity in the profession is maintained by the employers, knowing that students who have passed assessments have shown sufficient and substantial technical knowledge and application to a high standard.

Students are expected to not only show their knowledge but also to apply it in the context of the question and situation.

At higher levels in particular, assessment results are an indicator of not only your knowledge but professional skill and competence, and employers will want to know that you can undertake the task required to a high level of ability.

At every level, irrespective of the previous academic achievements of students, it should not be presumed that assessments will be easy, and students must prepare themselves as thoroughly as possible to be ready for the wide range of questions and question types that may occur.

There are numerous things that students can do when sitting an assessment to prepare as much as possible and to maximise the chances of success.

Before the Assessment

When preparing for the live assessments, it is worth being aware of the core ethical principles of the AAT, in particular the requirement for **professional competence and due care**. Professional competence is about having the knowledge and skills required, whereas due care is about taking care over revision and in the live assessment environment by reading the questions carefully and doing calculations with diligence.

One of the most important things that students can do to prepare for an assessment is to do as many practice questions as possible. AAT provide two practice assessments for each unit at every level. Training providers provide practice questions and publishing organisations such as Quo Vadimus Media Ltd provide practice questions for a good reason.

Practice questions are the best way of both solidifying your knowledge and practising the style of question and knowledge retrieval that AAT assessments demand. Practising a wide variety of topics through questions is the best way of preparing for an assessment. This is called retrieval practice, and it is vital to learning success.

When we learn a new skill or piece of knowledge, our brain will try to file it but is unsure where to put it, as it does not know yet how important that piece of knowledge will be in our future. By practising the retrieval of particular segments of knowledge through regular questioning, not only does that knowledge become more deeply embedded and secure, but our brain becomes more skilled at retrieving it, which helps in an assessment situation.

Practice questions, whether provided by AAT or organisations such as Quo Vadimus Media Ltd, have been proven by academic research to be more effective than revision methods such as re-reading notes or textbooks alone. Taking notes is important, and there is also plenty of research that suggests that even taking notes that are never read again will have some benefit over just listening or reading, but practice questions, and as many as students can get their hands on, is the best way forward.

Many students will choose to re-read their notes, textbooks or re-read PowerPoints or similar provided by training providers. These are useful if they form part of a larger revision strategy. If students however are choosing to re-read such items as a means of avoiding the (often harder mentally) practice questions available, it can backfire as students may be unprepared by the time of the assessment.

This does not however mean that reading is not important. One argument as to why students sometimes struggle in assessments is that they are not reading enough complicated pieces of text to be able to have the stamina and discipline to unpack complicated questions in the live assessment.

In terms of revision, little and often is also important. Do not just rely on a large cramming session just before the assessment. Short periods of 30 minutes daily, or even a few days a week, prior to an assessment will make a significant difference. For students who are studying in a classroom environment or online as part of a paced course, it is vital to study and practice the skills outside of the timetable.

As well as finding time to revise, finding space to revise is just as important. A place where studying can take place in peace is invaluable, and in the modern world, often hard to find. Particularly for those with families, finding the peace and quiet to study at home is difficult. However, a regular place or time to study, where a student knows that they are not likely to be disturbed, either at home, a place of work or a public location such as a library or coffee shop, can make a significant difference.

Familiarisation with practice assessments is vital, as it means the student understands how the assessment environment works before undertaking an assessment, so vital mental energy required to answer questions is not wasted on understanding how the assessment works.

Students should do each AAT-provided practice assessment at least once before the live assessment. Those assessments should be properly marked, by the student or a tutor, and the student should be aware of any errors that they made, rather than just relying on whether they are told they are competent or not yet competent. The feedback provided by the AAT software after a practice assessment is an invaluable tool for improving knowledge and skills.

Historically, according to anecdotal reports from students, AAT practice assessments have often been a little easier than live assessments, so students need to be wary that work still needs to be done, even if they have achieved well on practice assessments, as different and harder questions may be asked in the live assessment.

The AAT Examiner Report

For every unit in the Learning Portal, AAT provides an examiner report. This may seem like a dry and dull document that is of more use to tutors and training providers. However, it is a vital document that shows the common errors that students make on assessment tasks.

Common calculation errors are highlighted in the report and can give students valuable insight into the potential pitfalls in the assessment. The AAT examiner report highlights that the primary issue that students face in the exam tends to be attention to detail.

Although it is not revision because it does not provide subject knowledge, students should consider it a vital part of assessment preparation.

The examiner report provides valuable detail about common strengths and weaknesses in the live assessments and which tasks tend to be answered well or badly, providing useful areas of focus for revision.

During the Assessment

It should be obvious that students need a basic level of preparedness on the day of the assessment, including (but not limited to):

- An awareness of the assessment regulations.
- An awareness of any specific regulations or restrictions at the assessment venue.
- Check the calculator (and it should be a familiar one, it is not wise to use a calculator for the first time in an assessment).
- Writing materials (pen, pencils, etc.).

Being ready and feeling ready in practical ways will help in feeling more relaxed during the assessment and will help the memory remember key facts and knowledge than if stressed.

In the assessment itself, the following will increase student chances of success:

- Taking time – many students leave before the end of an assessment without having taken the proper time to answer the questions and check their work.

- Read every question thoroughly – a common error in all AAT assessments is not reading the question thoroughly or correctly. Students often answer the question they think that they are being asked rather than the one being asked. Resist the temptation to begin answering parts of the question until the whole question or task has been read.
- Check calculations – many errors are because students have not adequately checked their calculations. It is easy to enter incorrect numbers into the calculator or misread numbers on the screen. Ensure that each calculation is done at least twice.
- Do not leave a question unanswered, even if unsure – an empty box where there should be an answer is always a mark dropped, whereas even a best guess gives an opportunity for a mark gained.
- If a question is a struggle, come back to it later. It is understandable in an assessment situation for the mind to go blank or struggle with questions. Sometimes, moving on to another question and returning to it later can be beneficial.
- Check all work before clicking submit – do not just answer the questions, press submit and leave. Check through every question thoroughly.

AAT live assessments can be difficult, but the chances of success can be maximised by preparing thoroughly through revision and practice questions regarding key topics, familiarity with practice questions, and awareness and

Answers

Skills & Knowledge Test – Chapter 1

QUESTION 1

Identify the following as either cash or credit transactions by ticking the appropriate box.

	Cash Sale	Cash Purchase	Credit Sale	Credit Purchase
A sale where payment is required at a later date as indicated by its payment terms.			✓	
A purchase where immediate payment is required.		✓		
A purchase where payment is required at a later date as indicated by its payment terms.				✓
A sale where immediate payment is required.	✓			

QUESTION 2

Identify the purpose of each of these ledgers by ticking the appropriate box.

	Receivables Ledger	Payables Ledger	General Ledger
Contains the records of a number of different accounts for the business, dealing with a wide range of different transactions.			✓
Contains individual accounts for customers to whom the business sells on credit.	✓		
Contains individual accounts for suppliers from whom the business buys on credit.		✓	

QUESTION 3

Bookkeeping is part of.... *(tick as appropriate)*

Financial accounting	✓
Management accounting	

QUESTION 4

Identify the following by ticking the correct box.

	Ledger Accounts	Day books
The place where transactions are recorded or transferred to the double-entry accounting system.	✓	
Books which are used for recording the initial transactions regarding credit sales and credit purchases.		✓

QUESTION 5

Match the accounting category to the description by putting the correct answer in the box.
Options: *capital, drawings, asset, liability, expense, income, purchase*

Running costs of the business.	expense
An amount of money owed by the business to a third party.	liability
Money received from the sale of goods.	income
Money taken out of the business by the owner.	drawings
An item of value owned by the business.	asset
Money spent on buying raw materials or finished goods for resale.	purchase
Money put into the business by the owner.	capital

Skills & Knowledge Test – Chapter 2

QUESTION 5

For each of the following accounts, identify the account type.

	Asset	Liability	Income	Expense	Purchase	Capital
Money in the bank	✓					
Bank overdrawn		✓				
VAT owed by HMRC	✓					
VAT owed to HMRC		✓				
Money from sales			✓			
Buying raw materials					✓	
Rent paid				✓		
Rent received			✓			
Money paid in by owner						✓
Insurance payment				✓		
Computer equipment	✓					
Bank loan		✓				

QUESTION 6

For each of the accounts below, select whether it would normally have a debit or credit balance.

	Debit	Credit
Money in the bank	✓	
Bank overdrawn		✓
VAT owed by HMRC	✓	
VAT owed to HMRC		✓
Sales		✓
Purchases	✓	
Rent paid	✓	
Rent received		✓
Capital		✓
Insurance	✓	
Computer Equipment	✓	
Bank Loan		✓

QUESTION 7

Enter the following transaction into the double-entry records. The business has made a payment to the insurance company of £300. There is no VAT to consider.

Account	Amount £	Debit	Credit
Insurance	300.00	✓	
Bank	300.00		✓

QUESTION 8

Enter the following transaction into the double-entry records. The business owner has made drawings of £1000 from the bank.

Account	Amount £	Debit	Credit
Drawings	1,000.00	✓	
Bank	1,000.00		✓

QUESTION 9

Enter the following transaction into the double-entry records. The business has taken out a bank loan of £18,500.

Account	Amount £	Debit	Credit
Bank	18,500.00	✓	
Bank Loan	18,500.00		✓

QUESTION 10

Enter the following transaction into the double-entry records. The business has made a cash purchase of raw materials for £250 plus VAT.

Account	Amount £	Debit	Credit
Purchases	250.00	✓	
VAT	50.00	✓	
Bank	300.00		✓

QUESTION 11

For the following calculations of the accounting formula, assets minus liabilities equals capital, complete the table by filling in the blanks.

Assets	Liabilities	Capital
25,000	*12,750*	12,250
140,245	48,673	91,572
32,800	9,750	*23,050*
82,855	*41,855*	41,000
16,272	4,300	11,972
108,465	23,911	*84,554*

QUESTION 12

A business takes out a bank loan of £5,000. Which of the following will occur?

Assets will increase, liabilities will remain the same	
Liabilities will increase, assets will remain the same	
Assets will increase, liabilities will increase	✓

QUESTION 13

Identify whether each of the following transactions will be a credit or a debit in the bank account in the General Ledger.

	Debit	Credit
Payment of wages to employees		✓
Payment of insurance premium		✓
Receipt of money from sales	✓	
Money paid in by the owner	✓	
Money drawn out by the owner		✓
Payment of VAT bill to HMRC		✓
Receipt of VAT refund from HMRC	✓	
Payment of rent		✓
Bank loan received	✓	

QUESTION 14

Balance the following Receivables Ledger Control Account. *Note, you may have not seen this account yet, but this activity will still help you with your balancing skills, as well as introducing an account you will see in a subsequent chapter. The principles of balancing are identical to the examples seen in this chapter.*

Receivables Ledger Control Account					
Debit *(dr)*		£	Credit *(cr)*		£
02-01	Credit Sales	12,573	08-01	Money received	4.911
			31-01	Balance c/d	7,662
	Total	12,573	**Total**		12,573
01-04	Balance b/d	7,662			

QUESTION 15

Balance the following Payables Ledger Control Account. *Note, you may have not seen this account yet, but this activity will still help you with your balancing skills, as well as introducing an account you will see in a subsequent chapter. The principles of balancing are exactly the same as examples seen in this chapter.*

Payables Ledger Control Account					
Debit *(dr)*		£	Credit *(cr)*		£
14-01	Money Paid	11,100	08-01	Credit Purchases	21.284
15-01	Discounts received	969			
31-01	Balance c/d	9,215			
	Total	21,284	**Total**		21,284
			01-02	Balance b/d	9,215

QUESTION 16

Balance the following Wages Account.

Wages Account					
Debit *(dr)*		£	Credit *(cr)*		£
03-01	Wages	500	31-01	Balance c/d	1,500
10-01	Wages	500			
17-01	Wages	500			
	Total	1,500	**Total**		1,500
01-02	Balance b/d	1,500			

QUESTION 17

Balance the following Bank Account. *Note, this account is a little different, as it has an opening balance (b/f). It should be treated exactly as any other transaction and counted.*

Bank Account					
Debit *(dr)*		£	Credit *(cr)*		£
03-01	Balance b/f	2,500	03-01	Wages	500
04-01	Capital	1,211	09-01	Insurance	850
11-01	Sales	850	19-01	Wages	500
			31-01	Balance c/d	2,711
	Total	4,561	**Total**		4,561
01-02	Balance b/d	2,711			

Skills & Knowledge Test – Chapter 3

QUESTION 18

For each of the following net amounts, calculate the amount of VAT at 20% and the Gross total. All answers should be to the nearest pence and rounded down if appropriate.

Net £	VAT £	Total £
94.80	18.96	113.76
124.32	24.86	149.18
160.00	32.00	192.00
245.95	49.19	295.14
342.20	68.44	410.64
1235.60	247.12	1,482.72

QUESTION 19

For the following amounts that include VAT at 20%, calculate the net and the VAT. All amounts should be rounded down to the nearest pence.

Total £	Net £	VAT £
126.00	105.00	21.00
78.60	65.50	13.10
96.30	80.25	16.05
108.00	90.00	18.00
246.60	205.50	41.10
585.00	487.50	97.50

QUESTION 20

Record the following invoices in the Purchases Day book and then transfer the totals into the General Ledger and Payables Ledger. Account coding and balancing are not necessary.

Company	Date	Invoice no.	Price
Company A	01-02	Inv124	£100 exc. VAT
Company B	04-02	COBA12	£92 exc. VAT
Company C	05-02	GGA445	£476.20 exc. VAT

Purchases Day Book

Date	Details	Invoice no.	Net £	VAT £	Total £
01-02	Company A	Inv124	100.00	20.00	120.00
04-02	Company B	COBA12	92.00	18.40	110.40
05-02	Company C	GGA445	476.20	95.24	571.44
		TOTALS:	668.20	133.64	801.84

General Ledger

Account: Payables Ledger Control Account

Debit £		Credit £
	31-01 PDB	801.84

Account: Purchases

Debit £		Credit £
31-01 PDB	668.20	

Account: VAT

Debit £		Credit £
31-01 PDB	133.64	

Payables Ledger

Account: Company A			
Debit £			Credit £
	01-02	PDB	120.00

Account: Company B			
Debit £			Credit £
	04-02	PDB	110.40

Account: Company C			
Debit £			Credit £
	05-02	PDB	571.44

QUESTION 21

Record the following invoices in the Purchases Returns Day book and then transfer the totals into the General Ledger and Payables Ledger. Account coding and balancing are not necessary.

Company	**Date**	**Invoice no.**	**Price**
Company A	08-02	CN234	£8.60 exc. VAT
Company B	11-02	CN118	£43.60 exc. VAT
Company C	13-02	CC42	£274.20 exc. VAT

Purchases Returns Day Book					
Date	**Details**	**CN no.**	**Net £**	**VAT £**	**Total £**
08-02	Company A	CN234	8.60	1.72	10.32
11-02	Company B	CN118	43.60	8.72	52.32
13-02	Company C	CC42	274.20	54.84	329.04
		TOTALS:	326.40	65.28	391.68

General Ledger

Account: Payables Ledger Control Account					
Debit £					Credit £
28-02	PRDB	391.68			

Account: Purchases Returns					
Debit £					Credit £
			28-02	PRDB	326.40

Account: VAT					
Debit £					Credit £
			28-02	PRDB	65.28

Payables Ledger

Account: Company A					
Debit £					Credit £
08-02	PRDB	10.32			

Account: Company B					
Debit £					Credit £
11-02	PRDB	52.32			

Account: Company C					
Debit £					Credit £
12-02	PRDB	329.04			

QUESTION 22

Record the following invoices in the Discounts Received Day book and then transfer the totals into the General Ledger and Purchases Ledger. Account coding and balancing are not necessary.

Company	**Date**	**Invoice no.**	**Price**
Company A	11-02	CN18	£4.60 exc. VAT
Company B	19-02	CN431	£11.10 exc. VAT

Discounts Received Day Book					
Date	**Details**	**CN no.**	**Net £**	**VAT £**	**Total £**
11-02	Company A	CN16	4.60	0.92	5.52
19-02	Company B	CN431	11.10	2.22	13.32
		TOTALS:	15.70	3.14	18.84

General Ledger

Account: Payables Ledger Control Account	
Debit £	Credit £
28-02 DRDB 18.84	

Account: Discounts Received	
Debit £	Credit £
	28-02 DRDB 15.70

Account: VAT	
Debit £	Credit £
	28-02 DRDB 3.14

Payables Ledger

Account: Company A	
Debit £	Credit £
11-02 DRDB 5.52	

Account: Company B	
Debit £	Credit £
19-02 DRDB 13.32	

QUESTION 23

For the following invoice and PPD % amounts, calculate the amount of (gross) discount that can be taken, and the (gross) amount to be paid.

Invoice amount £	**% PPD**	**Discount to be taken £**	**Amount to be paid £**
200.00	5	10.00	190.00
150.00	2.5	3.75	146.25
450.00	4	18.00	432.00
620.00	10	62.00	558.00
180.00	6	10.80	169.20

QUESTION 24

The PPD discount amount (in £) should be deducted when calculating the initial value of an invoice.

True	
False	✓

QUESTION 25

A prompt payment discount of 5% on an invoice of 180.00 (inc. VAT) has been taken from a purchase from Company D.

What should be recorded in the General Ledger to record the discount?

Account	Amount	Debit	Credit
Payables Ledger Control Account	9.00	✓	
Discounts Received	7.50		✓
VAT	1.50		✓

What should be recorded in the Payables Ledger to record the discount only?

Account	Amount	Debit	Credit
Company D	9.00	✓	

What should be recorded in the General Ledger to record the payment actually made from the bank?

Account	Amount	Debit	Credit
Payables Ledger Control Account	171.00	✓	
Bank	171.00		✓

QUESTION 26

Match the statement to the ledger or account.

	Payables Ledger Control Account	Payables Ledger
Contains a summary of the transactions & balances of the supplier accounts.	✓	
Contains details of individual transactions and balances for individual suppliers.		✓

QUESTION 27

Identify the discount type from the description.

	Trade	Bulk	PPD
A discount offered if payment on the invoice is made within a certain time period.			✓
A discount % offered to a particular customer on all orders.	✓		
A discount offered for ordering more than a certain quantity or value of an item or items.		✓	

QUESTION 28

The following codes have been assigned to suppliers, assign correct codes to the new suppliers.

Harton PLC	HAR001
Booknorth Ltd	BOO001
Bood Supplies	BOO002
Dixon Supplies	DIX001

New supplier	Account Code
Ashburton Paper Supplies	ASH001
Harmfield Plastics	HAR002

Skills & Knowledge Test – Chapter 4

QUESTION 29

Record the following invoices in the Sales Day book and then transfer the totals into the General Ledger and Receivables Ledger. Account coding and balancing are not recessary.

Company	Date	Invoice no.	Price
Company D	08-02	INV001	£120 exc. VAT
Company E	11-02	INV002	£84 exc. VAT
Company F	19-02	INV003	£91.20 exc. VAT

Sales Day Book					
Date	**Details**	**Invoice no.**	**Net £**	**VAT £**	**Total £**
08-02	Company D	INV001	120.00	24.00	144.00
11-02	Company E	INV002	84.00	16.80	100.80
19-02	Company F	INV003	91.20	18.24	109.44
		TOTALS:	295.20	59.04	354.24

General Ledger

Account: Receivables Ledger Control Account	
Debit £	Credit £
28-02 SDB 354.24	

Account: Sales	
Debit £	Credit £
	28-02 SDB 295.20

Account: VAT	
Debit £	Credit £
	28-02 SDB 59.04

Receivables Ledger

Account: Company D	
Debit £	Credit £
08-02 SDB 144.00	

Account: Company E	
Debit £	Credit £
11-02 SDB 100.80	

Account:	
Debit £	Credit £
19-02 SDB 109.44	

QUESTION 30

Record the following invoices in the Sales Returns Day book and then transfer the totals into the General Ledger and Receivables Ledger. Account coding and balancing are not necessary.

Company	Date	Invoice no.	Price
Company D	14-02	CN001	£7.40 exc. VAT
Company E	17-02	CN002	£11 exc. VAT
Company F	18-02	CN003	£44.20 exc. VAT

Sales Returns Day Book					
Date	**Details**	**CN no.**	**Net £**	**VAT £**	**Total £**
14-02	Company D	CN001	7.40	1.48	8.88
17-02	Company E	CN002	11.00	2.20	13.20
18-02	Company F	CN003	44.20	8.84	53.04
		TOTALS:	62.60	12.52	75.12

General Ledger

Account: Receivables Ledger Control Account					
Debit £					Credit £
			28-02	SRDB	75.12

Account: Sales Return					
Debit £					Credit £
28-02	SRDB	62.60			

Account: VAT					
Debit £					Credit £
28-02	SRDB	12.52			

Receivables Ledger

Account: Company D			
Debit £			Credit £
	14-02	SRDB	8.88

Account: Company E			
Debit £			Credit £
	17-02	SRDB	13.20

Account: Company F			
Debit £			Credit £
	18-02	SRDB	53.04

QUESTION 31

Record the following invoices in the Discounts Allowed Day book and then transfer the totals into the General Ledger and Receivables Ledger. Account coding and balancing are not necessary.

Company	**Date**	**Invoice no.**	**Price**
Company D	24-02	CN004	£1.20 exc. VAT
Company E	26-02	CN005	£10.60 exc. VAT

Discounts Allowed Day Book					
Date	**Details**	**CN no.**	**Net £**	**VAT £**	**Total £**
24-02	Company D	CN004	1.20	0.24	1.44
26-02	Company E	CN005	10.60	2.12	12.72
		TOTALS:	11.80	2.36	14.16

General Ledger

Account: Receivables Ledger Control Account

Debit £			Credit £		
			28-02	DADB	14.16

Account: Discounts Allowed

Debit £			Credit £		
28-02	DADB	11.80			

Account: VAT

Debit £			Credit £		
28-02	DADB	2.36			

Receivables Ledger

Account: Company D

Debit £			Credit £		
			24-02	DADB	1.44

Account: Company E

Debit £			Credit £		
			26-02	DADB	12.72

QUESTION 32

For the following invoice and PPD % amounts, calculate the amount of (gross) discount that can be taken, and the (gross) amount to be received.

Invoice amount £	**% PPD**	**Discount to be taken £**	**Amount to be received £**
180.00	4	7.20	172.80
250.00	5	12.50	237.50
100.00	2.5	2.50	97.50
240.00	6	14.40	225.60
175.00	2	3.50	171.50

QUESTION 33

A prompt payment discount of 3% on an invoice of £280.00 (inc. VAT) has been taken from a sale to Company D.

What should be recorded in the General Ledger to record the discount?

Account	Amount	Debit	Credit
Receivables Ledger Control Account	8.40		✓
Discounts Allowed	7.00	✓	
VAT	1.40	✓	

What should be recorded in the Receivables Ledger?

Account	Amount	Debit	Credit
Company D	8.40		✓

What should be recorded in the General Ledger to record the payment actually received into the bank?

Account	Amount	Debit	Credit
Receivables Ledger Control Account	271.60		✓
Bank	271.60	✓	

QUESTION 34

Match the statement to the ledger or account.

	Receivables Ledger Control Account	Receivables Ledger
Contains a summary of the transactions & balances of the customer accounts.	✓	
Contains details of individual transactions and balances for individual customers.		✓

Skills & Knowledge Test – Chapter 5

QUESTION 35

A credit customer has just paid an invoice for £200 + VAT by bank transfer. What will be the correct entry in the Cash Book?

Credit the Bank column with £240, enter £240 in the Trade Receivables column, no entry in the VAT column.	
Credit the Bank column with £240, enter £200 in the Trade Receivables column, enter £40 in the VAT column.	
Debit the Bank column with £240, enter £240 in the Trade Receivables column, no entry in the VAT column.	✓
Debit the Bank column with £240, enter £200 in the Trade Receivables column, enter £40 in the VAT column.	

QUESTION 36

A credit supplier has just been paid £400 + VAT by bank transfer. What will be the correct entry in the Cash Book?

Credit the Bank column with £480, enter £480 in the Trade Payables column, no entry in the VAT column.	✓
Credit the Bank column with £480, enter £400 in the Trade Receivables column, enter £80 in the VAT column.	
Debit the Bank column with £480, enter £480 in the Trade Receivables column, no entry in the VAT column.	
Debit the Bank column with £480, enter £400 in the Trade Receivables column, enter £80 in the VAT column.	

QUESTION 37

You have made cash sales (in cash) of £150 + VAT in cash. What will be the correct entry in the Cash Book?

Debit the Cash column with £180, enter £150 in the Cash Sales column and £30 in the VAT column.	✓
Debit the Cash column with £180, enter £180 in the Cash Sales column, no entry in the VAT column.	
Credit the Cash column with £180, enter £150 in the Cash Sales column and £30 in the VAT column.	
Credit the Cash column with £180, enter £180 in the Cash Sales column, no entry in the VAT column.	

QUESTION 38

You have made cash purchases of £60 + VAT by cash. What will be the correct entry in the Cash Book?

Debit the Bank column with £60, enter £60 in the Cash Purchases column, no entry in the VAT column	
Credit the Bank column with £72, enter £60 in the Cash Purchases column and £12 in the VAT column	
Credit the Cash column with £72, enter £60 in the Cash Purchases column and £12 in the VAT column	✓
Credit the Cash column with £60, enter £60 in the Cash Purchases column, no entry in the VAT column	

QUESTION 39

Indicate for the following statements whether they are true or false.

	True	False
The Bank column of the Cash Book can be carried down on either side, depending on the balance.	✓	
The Cash column of the Cash Book can be carried down on either side, depending on the balance.		✓

QUESTION 40

The following items need to be added to the debit side of the Cash Book. Add them and then complete the Cash Book as appropriate and total each column.

£210 including VAT received from a credit customer, Company A, by bank transfer.

£300 including VAT received. This is £225 by cheque, £75 in cash for goods received today from Company B.

Cash Book

Details	Cash	Bank	VAT	Trade Receivables	Cash Sales
Balance b/d	276	1,456			
Company A		210		210	
Company B	75	225	50		250
Totals	351	1,891	50	210	250

The credit side of the cash book for the same period shows that there were payments of cash of £108. What is the cash balance?

243

The credit side of the Cash Book for the same period shows that there were payments of £283. What is the bank account balance?

1,608

Is the bank balance a debit or a credit balance in the Cash Book?

Debit	Credit
✓	

QUESTION 41

These are Cash Book totals for the end of the time period.

Cash £	Bank £	VAT £	Trade Receivables £	Cash Sales £	Cash £	Bank £	VAT £		Trade Payables £	Cash Purchases £
416	15881	----	983	----	614	15881	108		392	113

What will be the entries in the General Ledger?

Account	Amount £	Debit	Credit
Receivables Ledger Control Account	983.00		✓
VAT	108.00	✓	
Payables Ledger Control Account	392.00	✓	
Cash Purchases	113.00	✓	

QUESTION 42

Indicate whether the following payments or receipts will be recorded on the credit or debit side of the Cash Book.

Transaction	Debit	Credit
Payment to credit supplier		✓
Payment from credit customer	✓	
Bank interest received	✓	
Bank charges paid		✓
Cash sales	✓	
Cash purchases		✓
VAT on sales	✓	
VAT on purchases		✓

VAT on sales and VAT on purchases are analysed columns, the VAT will be recorded on the same side as the original entry in the Cash Book, with the VAT entries recorded on the opposite sides in the VAT Account in the General Ledger.

QUESTION 43

Indicate whether the following payments or receipts will be recorded in the Cash or Bank column of the Cash Book.

Transaction	Cash	Bank
A credit customer pays you in cash	✓	
A credit supplier is paid by cheque		✓
A cash purchase paid by debit card		✓
A cash sale paid by cheque		✓
Cash received for a cash sale	✓	

Skills & Knowledge Test – Chapter 6

QUESTION 44

Which of the following statements accurately describes the imprest system?

When the Petty Cash is topped up, it is always topped up to the same amount.	✓
When the Petty Cash is topped up, it is topped up to a different amount each time.	

QUESTION 45

All businesses use the imprest system, true or false?

True	False
	✓

QUESTION 46

The amount to which petty cash is topped up according to the imprest system may be set in company policies, true or false?

True	False
✓	

QUESTION 47

The Petty Cash Book began with an opening balance of £250.00. During the month there were payments of £132.87 and receipts of £11.00. What will be the double-entry required to restore the imprest from the Bank Account?

Account	**Amount £**	**Debit**	**Credit**
Petty Cash	121.87	✓	
Bank	121.87		✓

QUESTION 48

The Petty Cash Book began with an opening balance of £300.00. During the month there were payments of £192.16. What will be the double-entry required to restore the imprest from the cash held in the business?

Account	**Amount £**	**Debit**	**Credit**
Petty Cash	192.16	✓	
Cash	192.16		✓

QUESTION 49

The business restores its imprest to £200 on the first day of every month. These are the petty cash payments for one month.

Date	Details	Amount £	Date	Details	Amount £	VAT £	Office Supplies £	Travel £	Misc. expenses £
1 Nov	Bal b/d	200.00	4 Nov	Office	75.00	12.50	62.50		
				Travel	10.00			10.00	
				Misc.	66.00	11.00			55.00
				Travel	25.50			25.50	

What entry in the Petty Cash Book is required to restore the imprest from the bank ?

Details	Amount £	Debit	Credit
Bank	176.50	✓	

What will be the total of the VAT column in the Petty Cash Book? The £ symbol is not required.

23.50

QUESTION 50

Enter the following transactions into the Petty Cash Book and total the columns:

- January 4th - Supplies for the office, £125.00 (excluding VAT)
- January 5th - Train travel, £18.90 (no VAT)
- January 6th - Train travel, £21.50 (no VAT)
- January 8th - Book purchase, £19.00 (no VAT)

Total the columns on the credit side of the Petty Cash Book once complete.

Date	Details	Amount £	Date	Details	Amount £	VAT £	Office Supplies £	Travel £	Cash purchases £
1 Jan	Bal b/d	300.00	4 Jan	Office supplies	150.00	25.00	125.00		
			5 Jan	Train travel	18.90			18.90	
			6 Jan	Train travel	21.50			21.50	
			8 Jan	Book purchase	19.00				19.00
				Totals:	209.40	25.00	125.00	40.40	19.00

Transfer the totals to the General Ledger.

Account	Amount £	Debit	Credit
VAT	25.00	✓	
Office Supplies	125.00	✓	
Travel	40.40	✓	
Cash Purchases	19.00	✓	

What is the balance of the account (how much money is left in Petty Cash)? The £ symbol is not required.

90.60

1:1 Tutoring

Graeme Lamb is available for 1:1 tutoring, for:

- content tutoring
- content consolidation
- exam preparation
- exam strategies

Sessions are either 1 hour or 2 hours in length.

For further information, visit:

https://www.quovadimusmedia.co.uk/tutoring

Printed in Great Britain
by Amazon

60026581R00116